MW01123862

ANTHOLOGY

RISE UP

WOMEN WHO LEAD
BUILDING*LEGACY*

COMPILED BY

DR. NEPHETINA SERRANO

Table of Contents

Dedication

I dedicate this book to ALL the Women Leaders around the world who are influencers and trailblazers leading the way building legacy. Ladies on the frontlines and those leading the way from behind the scenes your presence is felt. This one's for YOU. Thank you to the many women who have gone before us and led by example, who have had to fight their way through life's trials, tribulations and have triumph to Victory. To Those women who are still fighting for us now and for our future generations of Queen Women Leaders. I encourage you to stay strong, know you are not alone and we are better together.

Sincerely,

Dr. Nephetina L. Serrano

Serrano Legacy Publishing, LLC

<u>Acknowledgments</u>

First and foremost, I would like to acknowledge God who has made this moment possible and is here with me now. He shows me every day that he loves me more than enough. Thank you Lord for being the center of my joy and constant force of all things good in my life. My savior and my deliver in whom I put my trust.

To my Husband and bestie, Minister, Dr. Richard Serrano, you are my biggest supporter always cheering me on. Thank you for loving all my crazy, for all the nights you go to bed without me, praying me through when things get overwhelming. I say thank you my forever love, you lead me in ways that you will never know. I am tremendously blessed to have you in my life. To our daughter Brande who has a smile that lights up a room. There is no step in my love for you, from the day I set eyes on you that sweet little girl, and well it was an instant bond we shared. I am happy God chose me to be your bonus mom and you are my forever Puddin. Praying that God always watch over you and life always treat you kindly.

Thank you to every woman who have influenced me along my life's journey. Starting with my Grandmother Emma (Mama) deceased, YOU loved me so much and I am so glad I was able to experience your love and your cooking, hence why I love cooking today. To my amazing 4x Degree earner, Mommy Emma Jean Brant M.A.C.C., You taught me never stop learning and it is never too late to begin again, Aunt Louise (aka aunt Loudi) for caring for me as your own daughter, you showed me how to be strong, take care of family and never give up, Auntie Quin who was my bestie growing up and always looking out for me, braiding my hair, making my clothes even now still rescuing me when I need it. Mom Pat (deceased) what can I say, you were love and you gave love, there was never stepchild in your vocabulary just daughter. You ladies showed it really does take a village to raise a family. I am everything I am because you all poured into me a little of you.

To my sisters' January, Tanya, and Rosie, you three are part of my why and I love each of you. My Brothers' Pastor Roosevelt Brant III, Hakim, and Tyre (Deceased) love you guys more than you know and Ty I miss you beyond words. My Nieces Tiffany and Alexiis, two beauties who take after their auntie LOL, never give up on your dreams always have a plan and never stop moving forward. BE THE ONE and always lead yourself first. My little bundle of joy the latest edition Ameii Love … you have brought Tio and I so much love thank you God. Love you Teti.

Note: A pause for me. I am so proud of myself after having two major surgeries God delivered this project to me and it has not been an easy assignment to carryout but when you are pregnant with purpose and destiny it is never going to be easy. I tell you do not abort your purpose go through the process let go and let GOD lead you. I am a witness He will even in the eleventh hour. God will not let you fail. He will send you people that will hold up your arms,

WOG; Di, Shannon, Kenise, Claudia, Juliet, January, Kearn, HRH Moradeun, Mom Tillman, Lorraine, Terry, Cynthia, Michelle, Staci and many others praying for me to succeed. People that will pray when you are not looking and willing workers that will jump in the water and not let you drawn. For every hater, God sends angels to carry you and when you are alone, you are not alone because God is your refuge and very present help in time of need. You will get through it and come out VICTORIOUS... He Promises us the Victory!

Now oh, to my spiritual family, MT Airy C.O.G.I.C. to my leaders Bishop J. Louis Felton and Lady Dr. Pricilla Felton I have learned a lot watching you. Overseer Bishop Ernest C. Morris Sr., and Mother Winifred Morris what can I say you are true leaders who lead and have built a legacy. You have taught me so much over the past 30 years and I am forever grateful for God putting you both in my life. My husband and I love you both for the Leaders you are and the example you have been, words cannot fully disclose what I feel inside for you and your family who have been family to us. Overseer Reginald Macon and Evangelist Terry Moragne-Macon thank you for leading yourselves first and sharing the love of God.

Wow. I certainly want to thank these amazing ELITE group of women who have risen up from the ashes of life's most despairing moments and have decided to not stay down, not stop but to RISE UP and move forward. These women who made a decision to not allow defeat to be an option for them. Thank you ladies for yielding a yes to this anthology, for your determination, representation and showing up for you first so that you can lead by example to the rest of the world. Showing the world and those to follow it is not how you start but how you finish. Each of you are making an impact into this world that will be felt, talked about, duplicated and celebrated long after we are gone. CONGRATULATIONS we are better TOGETHER!

RISE UP Women Who Lead Building Legacy!

Sincerely,

Dr. Nephetina L. Serrano
Serrano Legacy Publishing, LLC

SPECIAL THANKS TO THE FOLLOWING:

SHANNON JARRETT, SPEAK BEAUTIFUL – BOOK COVER, BACK DESIGN AND VIDEO, CLAUDIA CRAMER, CSC PROFESSIONAL EDITING & CREATIVE WRITING SERVICES (GHOST WRITING SPECIAL SERVICES), YOMI GARNETT, MD ROYAL BIOGRAPHICAL INSTITUTE - CONTRIBUTING EDITOR, ACE RANDAL 4GGRAFAX, INC. – COVER FLYER, DI CARTER - SOCIAL MEDIA GURU 10 DAY GRAPHIC DISPLAY, KENISE ETWARU LAYOUT & SUPPORT CARE, PHOTOGRAPHY BACK PHOTO BY JACKIE HICKS FOND MEMORIES PHOTOGRAPHY, MAKE –UP LETITIA THORNHILL, HAIR MICHELLE SCOFIELD

About Dr. Nephetina L. Serrano

Relationship Expert, *The* Marriage *CEO* ®

Dr. Nephetina Serrano is the Chief Publisher of **Serrano Legacy Publishing Co.**, she is a National and International Inspirational speaker, a determined, committed Influencer who is changing the game and making a difference in the lives of, women, girls and couples around the world.

Dr. Serrano is Co-Founder of Covenant Marriages, Inc., Covenant Rescue 911 a 24 hour hotline for couples and families in crisis and Covenant Marriages Institute. Co-Author of the Book, **"The Marriage Corporation"** and Publisher of **Marriage CEO Magazine** "For the Entrepreneur Who Leads, Building Legacy". Married to the love of her life and best friend, Dr. Richard Serrano for over 32 years with one daughter Brande Serrano. She is a Certified Counselor and member of National Biblical Counseling Association (N.B.C.A.), Certified Life Coach, 5x Best Selling

Author, and Mentor. She has mentored young women and girls within and outside her community. She has held positions of Board member and advisor mentor of KISH Home Inc., Big Brothers and Big Sisters, President of Young Women Christian Counsel and more.

Dr. Nephetina along with her husband Dr. Richard Serrano have an outside the four walls ministry, helping couples in transitional phases within their marriage while also providing a learning platform for singles preparing to embark on their own marital journey. Together they are working within their nonprofit organization, Covenant Rescue 911 501c3 24 hour hotline for couples and family in crisis. They are currently working to build a 72 hour overnight stay crisis facility.

*Dr. Serrano has received countless awards and certificates honoring and acknowledging her contributions to women and girls such as: City Council of Philadelphia CITATION. Women of Wealth, Publishers Golden Eagle Award, ACHI Magazine Woman of Inspiration Award 2019. **Success Magazine** named her as one of the **100 Best Life Coaches 2021**, State of California SENATE recognition in honor of GSFE Senator Richard D. Roth 31st District, California Legislature Assembly Game Changer Award, Assembly Member 61st District Jose Medina 2021, County of Riverside Influencer,* Catalyst for Change Girls with Pearls honoree. *Award and much more.*

Other Books includes:
*Make It Happen **#1 International Best Seller***
*The Price of Greatness **#1 Best Seller***
*No Matter What You Can Make It **#1 Best Seller***
*"RISE UP" Women Who Lead Building Legacy **#1 Best Seller & Best New Release***

DR. NEPHETINA L. SERRANO

www.marriageCEOs360.com

DrSerranoministries@gmail.com

116 BALA AVE, SUITE 1B, BALA CYNWYD, PA 19004

RISE UP – WOMEN WHO LEAD BUILDING LEGACY

<u>Endorsements</u>

"Establishing a strong legacy is a non-negotiable mandate in our endeavor to leave an indelible and unequivocal mark on the world while we still have breath in our bodies. Each new morning, we rise, challenging ourselves to answer the pivotal question: *How will we leave this earth empty while imparting a legacy of accomplishment to our industries, friends and loved ones?* RISE UP: Women Who Lead Building Legacy is a rare literary jewel, a dynamic anthology of 33 world changing, paradigm shifting women of honor. It is a premiere blueprint of legacy for us all, unmatched by any other book of the decade. Savor each story of triumph over insurmountable odds, soaking in the words of wisdom that will uplift your soul in the darkest soul-wrenching trials of life. Through the poignant transformative stories of these heroines of purpose, you will learn that defeat is yet a mere opportunity to fail forward, empowering the indomitable spirit within, authored by the Creator to *RISE UP* unapologetically into your greatness."

- **Les Brown**
Legendary Iconic Motivational Speaker

***

This book documents the journeys of 33 female visionaries across the globe who have used their personal hardships and obstacles to triumph and thrive in life, becoming some of the most influential voices in today's society. In each chapter, you will bear witness to the powerful force of perseverance and resilience, where women of triumph use their stories to inspire the champion inside of us all. Weaved so intricately in the stories of these trailblazers, I can't help but witness the sometimes unspoken but pivotal role of Yahweh (God) as He turns tears into triumph, hardship into healing and mishaps into miracles. This is a must read of hope needed for such a time as this!

- **Sister Perri aka Pebbles**
Founder of WOGCL & Miracle Mondays

***

As provoking as it is empowering, Anthology "Rise Up" Women Who Lead Building Legacy, glows with a sense of honest hope. 33 women, 33 stories that will bring tears, joy and a sense of purpose to every reader of this masterpiece. Dr. Nephetina Serrano, wonderfully followed her heart, flung her arms wide open and welcomed a heroic journey that will change lives forever.

- **Dr. Lauretta Pierce**
CEO/Founder Covenant Cookies Inc.

***

This is not a good book just because it is well written. It is a good book because it encourages and uplifts. More importantly, it speaks into a certain hope, even after the most devastating of life challenges. These coterie of women tell tales of despair. They tell tales that bring tears to the eyes. Their stories are as poignant as they are instructive. Ultimately, their stories teach us that, as a project, life can be very challenging indeed. This is an incontrovertible fact. Yet, once we gain intimate familiarity with, and accept that fact as a statement of our unavoidable reality, and then yield in total submission to the universal Will and abiding grace of God, the fact that life is challenging is no longer one to be celebrated, and having been robbed of its mystique, life becomes a much easier project to pursue. I congratulate Dr. Nephetina Serrano and her team of Amazons on this remarkable piece of work.

- **Yomi Garnett MD**
CEO, Royal Biographical Institute

FOREWORD

By: HRH Princess Dr. Moradeun Ogunlana
Founder of African Women's Health Project International
(AWPHI)

This trailblazing book is not only apt for the times, but its entrance into the global literary market is also quite timely. As I have always been thrilled with the importance of leaving a lasting legacy, the author Dr. Nephetina Serrano's invitation for me to say a few words on *RISE UP – WOMEN WHO LEAD BUILDING* left me only too honored and thrilled to do so.

Inspired by her extraordinarily successful RISE UP Facebook Streaming Series, Dr. Nephetina Serrano with her amazing change-agents, influential female authors that are redefining what it means for today's woman to take her destiny totally in her control and shape it with the quaint narrations that they speak. These amazing women, through their words, have succeeded in presenting us with a rendition of the all-empowered woman as she traverses her world with a sense of confidence and grace. The RISE-UP woman has cultivated a strong, yet generous heart, emanating the inner beauty that truly sets her apart. After reading this incredible, non-stop page-turning book, readers will come out with a newfound sense of direction and laser-focus instinct and control. With this book, the reader is empowered to rise from the ashes of despair and gloom, soaring to a new plane of existence that is totally free of limiting beliefs and tendencies.

Dr. Nephetina and her amazing change-agent authors inspire readers to refocus on the power within, skillfully integrating a healing balm to strengthen and restore holistically: the *whole* you and me. So now, her senses are refined; she sees and hears everything with clarity. That is why she can hear the wind rustling through the trees, beckoning her to live the dreams she holds so dearly. Having tasted the bitter and savored the sweet fruits of life, she has learnt how to overcome adversity and push past heartache and strife. Certainly, if there was one thing she never understood, and which she now knows to be true, it is that it all begins and ends with HER.

That is why, dear women who lead building, I join the author in asking you to RISE UP, and take your place as the queens that you indubitably are, insisting to be treated as such. For doesn't the Holy Book state clearly that as one thinks in her heart, so is *she?* (Proverbs 23:7) Indeed, you were destined for the great things of this life. Because of this, l ask you to resolutely refuse to be at the receiving end of, nor make do with the crumbs from the table of life. I ask you to step out regularly, and with bold confidence, re-establishing your claim to the inheritance of your Creator's kingdom. And your regal bearing will never be misconstrued as arrogance. For arrogance can only cast a shroud of insecurity. Life will give you only what you ask for: no more, no less.

I want to commend the incredible work that has gone into putting this book together, and I thank and congratulate my dear amazing Dr. Nephetina Serrano for inviting me to be a part of this masterful blend of spiritual wisdom, common sense, inspirational journeys and personal reflection.

All the Best!

HRH Princess Dr. Moradeun Ogunlana

Founder and CEO, African Women's Health Project International

THE GLOBAL SUMMIT GROUP INC

www.awhpi.org

www.princessmoradeun.com

www.globalcouncilofwomen.com

About HRH Princess Moradeun Ogunlana, Ph.D.

HRH Princess Dr. Moradeun Ogunlana is a visionary, entrepreneur, consultant, and humanitarian. As a recognized leader on women empowerment for Africa in the United States and around the world, the Princess is descended from one of the oldest and most distinguished Royal Family lines in Lagos, Nigeria.

Princess Moradeun is the Founder/CEO of African Women's Health Project International/ AWHPI Global Foundation, and President/CEO of the Innovative Global Consulting (IGC) Group of Companies. Additionally, The Princess is the official brand Ambassador of Adire Oodua Textiles under the Chairmanship of His Imperial Majesty, Oba Adeyeye Enitan Ogunwusi, OJAJA II - the Ooni of Ife, Nigeria - Africa's Foremost Monarch.

As the Founder/CEO of the African Women's Health Project International (AWHPI), she leads an international non-profit group that focuses on empowering women globally thru access to healthcare, economic empowerment, agriculture and trade associations, cultural developments, and partnerships.

In her capacity as the Chair of The Global Summit Group, Inc. - UN Global Compact participating member, she works on economic equity issues affecting women through groundbreaking research and training programs. Her commitment to women's economic empowerment has extended to the global arena, where she has provided an ongoing empowerment forum through the Global Council of Women for Development.

Long known for her coalition work, Princess Ogunlana has served on numerous boards of directors and advisory boards of nonprofits such as the Fight Cancer Global, Global Women Influencers Leading Transformation (GWILT), The GUIDE UK/UAE, Universal Peace Federation, Sino-Africa Economic Development Forum, and host of others. She serves as the Vice President of the Houston Abu Dhabi Sister Cities Association, and hosts the annual Global Women Empowerment Summit at the UN on business, agricultural, education, health and economic development issues. Most recently, she is named as the Brand Ambassador for FIDU Properties' INVEST IN DUBAI - AFRICA initiatives.

Princess Ogunlana's commitment to promoting citizen diplomacy through culture, nationally and internationally, stems from her decade-long involvement with the Sister Cities International, both as a commissioner and a global citizen.

Princess Ogunlana is the author of the bestselling book: The Achiever's Power - 50 Golden Nuggets to Becoming an Unstoppable Achiever. She is a graduate of the University of Arkansas at Little Rock, and has received numerous humanitarian awards, philanthropic commendations, and congressional citations, and most recently received the Governor's Excellence Award from the state of Arkansas.

The Princess lives between Arkansas, Texas and Nigeria.

C-A-N-C-E-R: A PERSONAL ENCOUNTER!

By: HRH Princess Moradeun Adedoyin-Solarin

C-A-N-C-E-R!!! The very word itself is taboo in some quarters, not to be mentioned or spoken of! For quite a while, the African woman has been faced with this killer disease, but we usually bury our heads in the sand like the proverbial ostrich, not taking into consideration the consequences of our actions. Research shows that lack of knowledge, medical care and adequate information have been the bane. For those living in the west, there is more awareness on the subject matter. As a result, women now pay more attention to their breasts and other body parts to help nip things in the bud.

Cancer is no respecter of persons; it does not announce that it's taking up residency in some part of your body. Most times it cleverly masks itself. But with the advent of continuous research and development of medical science, there are now simple ways and methods to detect cancer at very early stages, so it is quickly dealt with through medical treatment and if need be, quick surgery. Unfortunately some cases don't respond to treatment if the cancer has reached an advanced stage. As such it is very important that if changes are noticed in the breast or other parts of the body, seek medical opinion! Believe me, you will be doing yourself and your loved ones a big favor.

A Personal Encounter

I had a personal encounter with the dreaded 'C' some years ago, following the initial stages of fright, disbelief and ignoring the symptoms. After experiencing a dull pain and an abscess of fluids in my right mammary gland, I rushed to see my general physician who diagnosed it as an infection and treated it with a course of antibiotics. The pain and emission of fluid continued for nearly a year, then strange lumps appeared! Being in denial, I prayed and hoped these symptoms would go away; how wrong I was!

With support and encouragement from my husband, I decided to search the internet to find out all I could about this thing that had invaded my body! Eventually with enough information (thank God for the internet!), I gingerly got out of 'Camp Denial' and decided to deal with it squarely by seeking further medical advice from my general physician who then referred me to a male consultant. He was not sympathetic at all and told me curtly that I needed a mastectomy right away! He offered me no other options nor did he bother to explain things to me. I felt let down and frightened, and subsequently slipped into the 'it will go away' syndrome!

But when the symptoms became worse and unbearable, I went back to my general physician who scolded me for waiting so long and promptly referred me to another consultant. This time it was a female consultant, who kindly talked me through all I needed to know about cancer, explaining my condition in great detail, what was going on in my body and what had to be done. She booked me for surgery and treatment. I struck a deep friendship & sistah bond with my general physician thereafter.

I am eternally grateful that I was able to access information about cancer. I was also a recipient of a first-class treatment that through continuous research and development has been made available to women across the UK! I know I am really blessed to be in the clear and I thank God. I appreciate my husband, children, close family and friends for their love and support. My health has been good and I continue to live a wonderful life as a woman, wife, mother, grandmother and professional!

I advise that we all take note of any changes in our bodies and seek medical attention immediately when noticing even the slightest changes. Also, seek second opinions on everything. Don't be an ostrich; there is no such thing as 'it will go away'. We have just this one body and it is an original, so look after it well! Cosmetic or corrective surgery won't duplicate the real thing!

Updates
Much cancer research and development is and will continue to progress until this bane is finally eradicated from mankind! In Africa and some other parts of the world, cancer in women is still handled with kid gloves. Why you may ask? These factors come to mind:

Has The Covid-19 Pandemic Campaign Overshadowed it?

Our world was thrown into the Covid-19 Coronavirus Pandemic at the start of 2020. So while governments & health authorities were grappling with the task of finding cures and preventions for Covid, other serious ailments like cancer, HIV, etc. have been seemingly put on the back burner.

Lack of awareness in Government and Health Sectors?

HIV/AIDS as we all know, is an equally deadly disease with an alarming rise in the African continent. Because of the high level of awareness that has been achieved, everyone has a fairly good idea of what HIV/AIDS is, and the preventative steps to avoid contracting it. People also know what to do if treatment is needed and how to cope and live with it. Some governments are still grappling with campaigns and initiatives against cancer as a whole. They do not have the same kind of heavy campaign in place for it as they have for HIV/AIDS. Therefore if the governments don't have a clue, how will the general populace be informed?

Non-availability of Medical Personnel, Treatment and Facilities?

In places where there is cancer awareness, there is frequently inadequate medical personnel, drugs and equipment to combat it. This is really bad as most developing countries do not provide free or subsidized health care, and require patients to pay high and many times unaffordable prices for medical treatment. Due to this hardship, most folks just don't bother to go seek medical attention or treatment they cannot afford. They feel there is simply no point, a case of any which way but loose!

Cultural and Religious Factors?

Some indigenous cultures have deep-rooted cultural, religious beliefs and practices that can also be a big factor in these territories. In some cultures, such things are not to be brought up in discussion; it could be viewed as embarrassing to the family and could turn the woman into a pariah. From a religious standpoint, the factors can be quite convoluted depending on what side of the religious divide one is i.e. Traditionalist, Muslim, Jew, Christian, etc.

Scientists and medical practitioners around the world are determined to continue pressing on through scientific research and development for the battle against cancer. But as women, we also have roles to play in this struggle; it is rather a case of Each One, Touch One. We need to pay attention to our bodies and its functions. We must be informed about new discoveries and developments in these areas and be ready to share such information amongst ourselves.

It is proposed that women in developing nations where awareness of cancer and its treatment are still sparse, rise up as individuals & pressure groups to start lobbying governments though our constituencies and communities. We must ensure that our voices are not only heard, but heeded!

We must remember: "The hand that rocks the cradle rules the world." In effect, a lifeless hand cannot rock a cradle, let alone rule the world! So my sistahs, it's time to take the bull by the horns in affirmative action, as we continue to ARISE!

W.O.W. - Words of Wisdom

My grandmother, the Queen, always told us that to be born into royalty is a God-ordained privilege. Royalty is about leadership, and leadership is service to humanity. No one can tell the story of a place or a people as accurately as the people who have lived to tell the story. We must sit where they have sat, felt their pains, understand their struggles and challenges and embrace their achievements and successes to enable us to see things from their viewpoint.

There are stories that need to be told, wrongs to be righted, pertinent questions to be asked and answered; matters to be explained, legitimate claims to be made, people and achievements to be acknowledged, events to be celebrated, bridges to be built and of course, a journey of discovery and understanding to embark upon. On the same token, many issues affect women across the world, and our role is to arise! Finding lasting solutions must be our guest in building a United Nations of Womanity!

Princess Moradeun Adedoyin-Solarin is an authentic Yoruba princess of the Adedoyin Anoko Royal Lineage; the Grand Daughter of HRM Oba W C Adedoyin II, Akarigbo Anoko of Sagamu, Remo Kingdom, in Nigeria.

A Veteran Broadcaster, Seasoned Media Specialist, Project Management Consultant, Trainer, Mentor and sought after Professional. She is Operational Director Media and Communications of Global Women Inventors & Innovators Network (GlobalWIIN); Trustee Chair & Spokesperson Girl Child Network Worldwide (GCNW) & Girls Empowerment Initiative GEI, UK. Sits on Board of AFI World Peace Initiative NGIA (With UN ECOSOC Status); Board Member CEO Network & Royal Trustee/Advisor Economic Emancipation Movement (EEM) Bahamas; Ambassador, African Voice Magazine UK; Founder & Coordinator of The New Pan-African Movement (NPAM) & Founder League of Pan-African Royals (LOPAR). Her roles cover Communication & Media, Broadcasting, Community Development, Leadership, Mentorship, Training, and Empowerment.

https://about.me/hrhprincessmoradeun

A Tragic Experience Catapulted Me to Victory

By: Shirley Luu

* * *

Born in Vietnam, I came to the United States in 1974, the child of a Vietnamese mom who remarried an American G.I. after my biological father passed away during the war. I was raised in Maryland and later moved to Virginia, where I eventually married and raised a family.

In the initial phases of my professional career, I honed my skills in the telecommunications industry. With an interest in making and spending money, fate led me to a financial services presentation. That presentation opened a door for me to explore brand new opportunities so richly suited to my passions, skills and interests. It was in this presentation that I not only discovered how to prepare for my own financial future, but also realized that perhaps this was where my heart belonged.

I fell in love with the industry and began working part-time while still working full-time at my other job. It wasn't long before I began realizing six figures a year on a part-time basis. It was then that the light bulb went off. In fact, I prayed that I would get laid off at my telecommunications job. Interestingly, I actually survived three layoffs during that time.

I ultimately tendered my resignation and pursued my dream full-time. I began my new career within the mortgage industry and skyrocketed to success at seemingly warp speed, partnering with a firm and at one point overseeing 8,000 loan officers across the country. But then fate stepped in yet again, in a tragic way, tossing a huge emotional stumbling block onto my path. This tragedy would prove to give me the courage to turn it into a stepping stone.

That tragedy was the unexpected death of my husband 17 years ago. I vividly recall that fateful night being faced with some very tough decisions that I was forced to make. I had to lean on my unwavering courage and faith. As a single mom, I realized my options were limited at the time. Overnight my whole world was shattered, and I became a widow. At this point I was immersed in the mortgage industry, but as the economy was facing its historic decline, causing the mortgage industry to all but lose its footing, I knew I had to embrace a new direction to be able to provide for myself and my three children, then ages one, 15, and 16. Upon the night of the tragedy, instantly we were faced with homelessness and a life we had never known before. There was no time for me to sit around and overly bemoan my new status in life. Time was of the essence and I had to begin to act quickly. I had to make a decision to do it for my kids. If not, who would? Or, I could just sit there and feel sorry for myself and my family. People would have listened and sympathized, and then moved on to their own problems.

I instinctively knew one thing for certain: life is a roll of the dice at times, and challenging times do not discriminate. At any time, any one of us can be faced with homelessness due to an unexpected and devastating event, and if one does not proactively plan with respect to savings, retirement, and most importantly, life insurance, the prospect for turning it all around is bleak, at best.

This is where my newly found passion came into play and began to take center stage, turning my tragedy into triumph. I wrote my vision based on my passion and pursued it relentlessly, not stopping until my vision became a reality. My vision has now expanded beyond my wildest dreams.

Pulling on my love for helping and working with people, I poured myself into educating others, especially empowering women. I didn't want any other woman to ever have to suffer hardship the way that I had, especially when it came to preparing financially for retirement or other unforeseen events. There are so many statistics regarding the adverse impacts of being financially ill-prepared for life changes, and I can personally attest to how important it is to be financially literate. With two out of three American families lacking an emergency fund, I learned firsthand via personal hardships as my deceased husband had allowed his insurance policy to lapse.

I began to study the insurance industry and eventually began preaching it to others. I was most notably excited about the Indexed Annuity, which is a combination of a fixed and a variable annuity, essentially providing the best of both worlds, giving investors the low-risk appeal that comes with a guaranteed minimum return. I also focused on the new Indexed Universal Life

Insurance plans from which the owners of those plans can access benefits while still living. I realized that these products were cutting edge and the next generation of products.

Mastering my skills and helping thousands of individuals and businesses, I became the CEO of Shirley Luu and Associates, located in the heart of McLean, Virginia, with more than 4,000 agents across the country. How I did it is no secret:

1. I refused to allow tragedy to define or limit me.
2. Fear had no place in the pursuit of my passion.
3. I kept my "why" before me: my three children who were depending on me.
4. Hard work and service to others pushed me to do more.
5. Helping others in need along the way were the seeds that I sowed to nourish my garden of success.
6. I never gave up – quitting was never an option and each milestone achieved was a stepping stone to the next.
7. Team expansion demonstrated again and again that we are stronger together.
8. Leave a legacy.

Consistent with my passion to serve people, I am actively engaged in community outreach work, and chief among that mission is The LiSA Project, a grassroots movement founded by Debbie Gerlicher of First Financial Security, designed to inform, educate and empower women and their families with respect to financial security.

This project is near and dear to my heart as I know all too well that it is not a matter of IF one will be solely responsible for his or her finances, but WHEN. Through The LiSA Project, women are given the confidence to take stock of what they currently have financially, and are led on the path to take control of their financial health. I literally thrive off of helping others. I can't sit still for I was born to do this work. I believe it is our responsibility to give back to the community.

Today, my team of brokerage consists of 4000 agents spanning across 50 states, and 80% are minorities. I am also a bestselling author on Amazon for Retirement Planning and Life Insurance. And speaking of triumphs, I am part of a TV pilot show, "Overcomer". Overcomer is a story of helping five single mothers to overcome their financial struggles, which is a perfect fit as it aligns my passion with that which I have overcome.

W.O.W. – Words of Wisdom

I always wanted to be somebody. If I made it, it's half because I was game enough to take a lot of punishment along the way and half because there were a lot of people who cared enough to help me.

- Althea Gibson

Be tenacious, unwavering in pursuit of your passion. If you have a setback, you can come back!

Dr. Shirley Luu is an Award-winning financial advisor, trainer, author, national speaker, and renowned wealth guru. Her 25 expert years in financial services sets her apart as one of the industry's most notable connoisseurs.

An Executive Field Chairman for First Financial Security, Shirley Luu has dedicated over 25 years to informing, educating, and empowering individuals and small and large business owners on the most powerful mediums for lifetime income and retirement.

With the new branding "Shirley Luu & Associates, LLC," Shirley and her team of licensed professionals continue to configure the best financial and insurance products to serve each client's specific financial security needs. Her personal journey as a widowed mother of three, allows her to recognize the unique challenges that exist for women. She actively empowers women across the globe to "know their money" through various educational and enrichment programs, including the LiSA Initiative.

Triumph Behind the Crown

By: Jackeline Cacho

* * *

In life, we wear many hats; when opportunity and preparation meet, many of our hats may turn into crowns. I was once a beauty pageant queen. My hard work in the field of Communications resulted in me being crowned Queen of Edutainment in Spanish language programming in the United States. I am an international award-winning journalist. I have had the opportunity to speak all over the world. I am a two-time Emmy award nominee for my national independent television show, "Jackeline Cacho Presenta Triunfo Latino". All these crowns I use to serve those around me. However, many don't get to see the trials and inner battles I've faced before and between crowns. Allow me to share some of my story.

For me, it all began in my native land, Peru. In my twenties, I found myself modeling and was able to land some pretty major contracts. Between the big lights and the makeup, everything seemed beautiful and perfect on the outside, but somehow the glitz and glamour didn't make me feel like "me". I would go on to be offered a trip to New York and to audition for photo shoots with Sports Illustrated and other large companies. But amidst all of the opportunities and success, I found myself going for walks all alone, crying out to God, *Is this the way for me? I am not happy here and I cannot continue like this because I feel like I am suffocating!*

To add to my confusion and inner turmoil, one of the friends with whom I had shared several modeling gigs had recently died of a cocaine overdose. I was devastated and knew that was the sign I needed to take some time, reflect and regroup. I decided to leave town. And so, I moved to Houston, Texas.

My soul was aching and the voice inside me repeated, "Seek to find your true passion!" I knew perfectly well which direction I wanted my life to take. I knew how to position myself in the industry in such a way that opportunities would present themselves to me, even in Houston. I thank God and my father who made it a point to nurture a strong spiritual foundation within me. For that reason, although I felt alone, I never let myself be pulled into the underworld of modeling and celebrity, which can often be deceiving and a total sham. I was always aware that there was an expiration date to the fame, to that fast and fabulous life; all races have a finish line and staying in the race would require a ton of sacrifice. However, I would never sacrifice my spirit or my soul.

I worked three jobs, and was able to prove that I was indeed, a dutiful US citizen. My ultimate goal was to bring my whole family from Peru to the States. It was my motivation, my goal, my fight. I didn't mind sleeping only three and a half hours a day, nor did I mind having to sleep in a truck on my lunch break on my way to Telemundo. It didn't matter what I went through because I had a goal, and my goals helped me to push through the difficulties of life. It seemed I'd always had a little "Jiminy Cricket" in my pocket, prompting me to look for new opportunities. I knew they were looking for presenters for Univision and I decided to send my presentation video to their offices, a goal I had before I decided to move from Houston to Miami.

You can do this, Jackie. You can do this, Jackie, I told myself. My confidence had a lot to do with the fact that it was 1999 and I wanted to start the new millennium "the year 2000" with all the momentum I had. Thanks to the advice of my dear friend Bob Perry, I went on to send my demo tape to five affiliated stations of Univisión, the largest Spanish-language network in the United States: to Dallas, San Antonio, San Francisco, Laredo and New York. They called me and made me fly to three of those places before I had to decide to leave everything behind.

Around this time, I was able to bring my family to the United States, fulfilling a major goal of mine. This milestone was proof that I never gave up, I pursued my goals and with a lot of work and through much strife, I was able to manifest my dreams into reality. It was not easy, but my story is proof that it is doable.

When the Univision opportunity - for me, the opportunity of a lifetime - came, I hesitated at first. How could I get up and go when I had just invited my family to visit and live with me? My mother, always one to support my ambitions no matter how grand, encouraged me to keep on going. She understood and continues to understand the importance of fulfilling my goals. She knew that I had made it this far, working three jobs, obtaining citizenship, proceeding to bring my family members to the United States and still having goals that I wanted to accomplish. This opportunity, like many that I encountered, seemed prestigious and lucrative at the time. It did, however, come with some setbacks. "Mi hija, everything that glitters is not gold," -- I could hear that reminder coming from my mom, inside my head! After landing the job, I learned that the environment at the station where I worked was not the most pleasant. In fact, it was quite toxic at times. As a "newbie", I was made to feel inferior by members of the station's team who were senior to me and had been working there for years. The level of competitiveness was something I had never experienced before. In the workplace, women can sometimes harness feelings of jealousy or envy, sending off negative vibes instead of embracing opportunities for collaboration and teamwork. These "vibras" definitely affected me.

On camera, however, you would not be able to tell I was grappling with feelings of resentment, inadequacy and pain behind the scenes. Carrying that emotional weight on my back was very trying, and was only a part of the trauma that I had undergone up until that point. Later on, there would be days when I would get denied auditions or when job prospects would not go as planned. In those times, I had to shift my focus and make a conscious decision to reflect only on the positive things that I did have in my life.

And then the unexpected happened. One fateful New Year's Eve, I suddenly lost control of my car in plain daylight and was involved in a four-car collision. That was the day my life changed, without a doubt. I always say that was the day one part of me died and a new being of light was born in its place. I was rescued by an angel and for that I am extremely grateful. I am thankful that God sent this angel to save me. This was a wake-up call and turning point of my life. It helped me find purpose. There was a long healing process that ensued after the accident. However, after recovering, I was more than ever determined to pursue my purpose and passion in life, cherishing every moment of which God had gifted to me.

Sharing my story has been very therapeutic and makes up the final stage of the healing process for me. If there are other people who can heal through reading what I have shared in these pages, then I hope that they too can see that you can touch the depths of despair, and still find the light. There will always be a force from beyond that helps you and a God that reminds you with a whisper that you have a serious mission in life and that you are here to fulfill that mission.

This is something that I find occurs frequently, because my life has been difficult like that for many immigrants, like many women who have been alone, who have fallen and who have lost everything; I see that despite everything they have returned to fight and have made a victorious comeback. I have been very blessed and fortunate because God has always put wonderful people in my path who have trusted me. Doors have opened to me when I have gone knocking on them. I recognize, especially after arriving in this country that, here if you fight, commit yourself and work hard, you can make it. It's not easy, but it's possible!

Daily, on my programs either online or on television, I am blessed to come across the stories of so many of whom have all come a long way on their journeys - as mothers, as immigrants, as a new generation of valiant fighters - and this chapter is my way of sharing my story with you and ensuring that our legacy of strength and courage lives on for generations to come. Sometimes the trials and challenges we face in life make us stronger. If this successful Latina leader was able to RISE UP after being down, then you too can

40

definitely RISE UP and bounce better and stronger than ever before. Each experience is a challenge to give up or triumph, gaining the crown of achievement in lieu of the obstacles. You can do it!

W.O.W. - Words of Wisdom

*   *   *

Allow me to share with you one of my favorite passages, which I recite at many conferences:

God is our refuge and strength, a very present help in trouble. The reality is that there will be difficult times, but God promises to be our refuge. God has not failed us. He has promised to be with us in the middle of tragedy.

\-   Psalm 46:1-7

In reading about my internal struggles and the ways I overcame them, I hope women especially can find comfort in knowing that they are not battling the symptoms of anxiety alone.

BENDICIONES A CADA UNO DE USTEDES! Blessings to each and every one of you!

A portion of the content included in this chapter has been adapted with permission from the author from "My Emotional Backpack | How I Learned to Combat Anxiety and Panic Attacks" (Mi Mochila Emocional)

Jackeline Cacho is a Multimedia Influencer, and creator of the Edutainment Movement in Spanish programming in United States, award winning journalist Jackeline Cacho is making headlines with her 2-time EMMY Nominated National TV Show, celebrating 10 Years inspiring our Latino community around the country. She is also host and producer of her own weekly TV show, "Jackeline Cacho Presenta Triunfo Latino," which is aired across 20 of the most important Latino markets in the USA on the VME TV network, and every week through her social media platforms.

Her autobiography, **"Mi Mochila Emocional,"** has been selected for the Good Reading Section of the prestigious magazine "People en Español." Ambassador "Spotlight Champion" for United Nations, the European Union and World-renowned motivational Speaker. She is recipient of numerous awards, including "2019 Entrepreneur of the Month" award from the Latinas in Business Organization, New Jersey, and "Woman of the Year in Media 2016" by US Congress represented by Congresswoman Loretta Sanchez.

www.jackelinecacho.com

Leave A Legacy for Your Lineage "It's Time"

By: Dr. Renee Allen "The People's Choice Emcee"

* * *

In my lifetime, I have never witnessed the playing field being as leveled as it is right now! The pandemic has hit the restart button on America. This is the time to start your legacy or pick up the pieces and continue to BUILD Legacy for yourself and for many generations to come.

Being the oldest of three daughters, I was the one who was held accountable for the overall well-being of my sisters, and I loved them immensely. In hindsight, I would have enjoyed more time with my siblings however, I was always interested in being around older girls in school, as well as becoming friends with my parents' friends' daughters who were older than me.

In school, I connected well with people and became a leader amongst my peers. I participated in nearly everything that involved lots of people. It started with home talent shows for our family, then singing the lead solo in third grade (*Ben* by Michael Jackson) as well as many solos throughout the years; to winning the high school gong show with my sister Lisa and her best friend, who were back-up singers, as I sang lead to "Best of my Love" by the Emotions. I was the headliner in school plays (*Up the Down Staircase* and *Gypsy*), where I was scouted by the Greenwich Connecticut Repertory Theater and then became the first African American female "All

44

School Congress President" of my senior high school class. At one point, I remember there being an issue of principle going on in the school, and I rallied a group to protest. Most of the school followed a few of us onto the front lawn of the school for hours. I was an influencer and didn't realize my power of influence until that moment.

I have always yearned to explore and learn more about the world, so I joined the United States Navy right out of high school at seventeen years of age. I would go on to retire later in life with 22 years of honorable and highly decorated service. I am proud of this country and give a continued hand-salute to every veteran who ever served this beautiful nation.

Every day I strive for excellence! My mind is always on fire because there are so many opportunities at my fingertips, and I want to accomplish so much! However, there have been many detours in my life; nothing outweighs the divorce that tried to kill me! We were two people who found love, married and were making great money. We purchased a home, had a child, purchased timeshares and had two Mercedes vehicles in the garage; I felt like we had made it! I was the happiest woman in the world until we started having problems communicating with each other and not working as a team.

I wanted more children, but he was done! I wanted to work from home to be with our child while he was young. He didn't want a nanny to help while I worked in the house! I wanted romance, and he wanted a roommate (so it seemed)! We quickly became distant, and that's when my world came tumbling down. It was the worst experience ever, loving someone who behaved like an enemy!

After the separation, I would go through my day feeling like I was in slow motion and, once the courthouse ordeal started, it seemed to drag on forever. I was totally depressed and felt sad for our son because he was in the middle. He suffered profusely, and I still have feelings of guilt that I wasn't able to shield him from it. That whole ordeal haunted me like a dark shadow. At one time, I laid in bed, and, if it wasn't for my child, I don't think I would have ever gotten up. But God stepped in and intervened.

One day, I was in my kitchen, and somehow, I ended up on the floor under my double oven, weeping and humming a tune. I heard a voice say, *Get up, and get a pen and paper*. I started to jot the words on paper, and, a few hours later, I had written a song, "Lord Help Me," which my *sista* friend (the late) Sheila Stewart from Radio One scheduled me to sing for women in church and other venues. That song got me through the most horrible time of my life. You see, I never wanted a divorce, and it took over my life until I started helping others through music! It was the act of service to others that rescued me -- Glory to GOD!

To tell you the truth, at times, I feel I am still recovering from the devastation of the divorce. However, in life, you must be an overcomer through the roughest tests and toughest obstacles. Throughout my life, I have also been blessed to work in five mainstream industries, and I was able to retire in two of them. In all this, one thing was clear: you cannot build a legacy in a job as an employee. I am not *knocking* having a job. I just think that it may be a good idea to build something on your own time and when you match your salary, then it just may be a good time to become an entrepreneur full-time to receive all the write-offs and tax breaks. Just saying! Legacy requires blood, sweat and tears. Oh, did I mention heart and long hours? If you are building a business, it will take all that you have to succeed!

You, too, have all that you need to accomplish what you want! As long as you have a spark of a vision, you can make it happen! For as long as I can remember, my dad, Leith Douglas Fraser, always said, "Always smile, and they will never know what you're thinking." You must learn how to smile through the pain of growing your legacy! Life is not going to drop a legacy in your lap. Even if you receive an inheritance, you must learn the rules and tax laws or pay someone to run a trust for you in order to keep it.

Legacy starts with you! I am proud of my ancestors, my (late) Great-Grandma Annie, my (late) Grandma Connie, my (late) Aunt Pookie; I stand on their shoulders! They were phenomenal role models and amazing human beings who loved immensely and provided everything they had to protect and love their families! My mother especially continues to be an absolutely amazing woman that many admire. I thank God every day for assigning her as my mother and best friend! Ms. Charlotte Fraser drives my motivation to be our family's Legacy Maker. I am even so proud of my future Legacy Maker, my son, who at 19 has left a legacy by publishing a few of his thought-provoking poems during the pandemic and becoming an author!

If you do not already have a Legacy Maker in your family, then you must do it! It's up to you so that your family and future generations to come will be able to thrive versus just trying to stay alive. One of the best ways to secure a legacy, in my opinion, is investing in real estate, insurance or a business where you receive residuals by helping others get what they want so that you also get what you want!

One of the very few things that I absolutely love about social media is that you can "surf and see," getting visuals of the things you want in your life. There are a million ways to create what you envision and to learn how to do anything that your heart desires. You can do it, and I am cheering for you. Go for it! It is time.

W.O.W. - Words of Wisdom

* * *

Life is ultimately what you make of it! It is NEVER too late to build a legacy!

Here are a few tips to keep in mind:

1. Take the time to seriously think about what you want your family legacy to be.
2. Strategize so you will make the right choices for growth.
3. Act and walk as if you already have what you desire with humility.
4. Always remember your WHY and stay focused.
5. Do not cut corners or deliberately hurt anyone in the process.
6. Ensure that your paperwork is in good standing. You should have a will and any additional documents you and your business may need.
7. Build with your children's, children's children in mind and include your family in the process.
8. Serve to the very best of your ability and allow others who are capable to support you.

Dr. Renee´ Starlynn Allen is Host of the Renee´ Allen & Friends Show, and Co-Host of the Chris Thomas Show. She uses her platforms to connect like-minded, talented and extraordinary people. She is committed to educating, inspiring and empowering women, men and children. Featured in the second edition of Who's Who in Black Washington, DC, she is an international best-selling author. As Vice President of Media, Global Health Solutions (GHS), she is a UN Ambassador for Health and Human Trafficking.

A highly decorated twenty two-year veteran who served during the Grenada Invasion and Desert Shield/ Desert Storm. A proud mother of one amazing son, she is Historian & Secretary, Sisters 4 Sisters Network, Inc., and she sits on the Boards of several organizations.

ReneeAllenandFriends@gmail.com
IG: @ThePeoplesEmcee
FB: DrRenee Allen or Renee Starlynn Allen
Web site: www.DrReneeAllen.com

BITTER OR BETTER?

By: Marlena Martin

Sometimes life throws you a curve ball and you are ready for it. You laugh and say to yourself: *Been there, done that. I've got this one covered.* Other times, life will throw you a situation that you are ill-prepared to handle in every possible way. A moment in time so unexpected that it will forever change the course of your life.

* * *

In my mid-twenties, I got engaged. We met in Las Vegas. I had won a pageant there and was attending university at UNLV. He came into one of our local restaurants after a night of fun with his friends and we were seated across from each other. Once we said a few words in passing and realized we were both from San Diego, it was on. We were joking and sharing stories of our hometown during the entire meal. Once I stood up to leave, he asked for my number. This chance encounter was about to turn into so much more.

As most couples do, we started calling, talking on the phone almost nightly. We were long distance but not so far that we didn't start going on dates, driving to each other and spending weekends together to be with each other's friends and families to attend events. He was a great guy. A teacher. Kind-hearted. 100% in pursuit. Things were great from the very beginning. Everything was smooth in the relationship. Eventually he asked me to prepare to move to

San Diego. My parents were thrilled. I was finally coming home. And I adored his parents.

I really loved the tradition his family held at their house. Every Sunday they had a big family dinner. All the kid's growth spurts would be marked with a ruler on one of the columns leading into the kitchen. Right before eating, we would stand in the living room, forming a huge circle with his parents, siblings and any friends who happened to be over, to hold hands and pray before eating. I felt secure in that house. You could feel the love and support of everyone. It felt as if there was a safety net under us all. A house full of love and understanding. His larger family soon became the family I missed growing up as an only child. His brothers became my brothers. I went with him to their football games. Holidays and special events were marked by all of us in attendance.

My parents knew we would get married before he even asked. My mom told me one day, "He's the one." A month later, he proposed. Life was good. We had our inside jokes. Left little messages for each other, sent funny things in the mail that only the two of us would understand. He went to my high school reunion. We spent most of the time chatting outside, sitting by Mission Bay, the moonlight dancing on the water in our own special world. We were connected on a soul level. He had all the missing pieces that would solidify my life as a life partner, and it was beautiful to see the relationship between us and our families bloom. I was by his side as he advanced in his career, going from substitute teaching to a full-time coaching position at a local high school and eventually Vice Principal. I got offered a great job in Los Angeles but turned it down as we were planning to get married, and he wanted me to stop commuting and move to San Diego to prepare.

Right as I was embarking on a new entrepreneurial job, arranging the move and still six months out from the wedding, the beautiful life we had shared, built, prepared for, started to unravel. First, he started making large purchases which was out of character since we were saving for the marriage. Younger, immature friends then started whispering in his ear: "This is the beginning of the end! Once you are married man, the fun times are over!" He started going out late, partying with his single friends and arriving late to our dates. Whenever I asked him about it, arguments ensued. The doubt got stronger as he listened to his single friends. All of this probably could have been fixed. But then we suffered the deadliest attack of all. Another woman wanted him and was quite aggressive in her pursuit. She knew he was engaged, but she didn't care. She was determined. He became confused in the onslaught. Torn. Worst of all: in record time, he became unrecognizable from the man I had known.

In a matter of months, all that I had planned for was stripped away. I had a wedding dress, a wedding date, a reception booked, but now, no husband.

I had lost his siblings.

I had lost his parents.

I had lost my job.

I had lost my best friend.

I had no fiancé.

* * *

To say that I was ill-prepared for this was an understatement. To see my soulmate, the guy who worked so hard to earn my trust and love, gone? The guy of the inside jokes, the support and the nightly phone calls- gone? The dreams, the excitement? Gone. The deposits gone, the hope gone, my future as I had planned it. Vanished.

The entire situation was so overwhelming, I knew instinctively that I did not possess the tools to cope. I knew at that moment that I did not have enough life experience to handle the situation. What made matters worse was the well-meaning friends who said, "Aren't you glad you found out now?" or "You'll get over it—find someone else." It was as if folks were handing me Band-Aids when half of my body has been blown away in a grenade accident. It was like I lost half of my life, and I had major bleeding. I was Humpty Dumpty in the great fall and my entire life was shattered. I cried all the way to work. I cried on my lunch break. I cried on the way home. I even cried in lines standing to order food. I lost my sense of smell entirely. I would be two years later when I could smell again. I ate food but still lost weight. Nothing would stick. My parents were no help. They were angry at him, the situation and provided extraordinarily little emotional or spiritual support due to their own upbringings and life paths.

I was completely on my own. Utterly flattened and woefully unprepared. It would take a few years to recover from that experience, but here are the lessons I learned:

1. **Will I be BITTER or BETTER?** I knew I could use this to grow me or sour me. I decided, though in a lot of pain at the time, to allow this to make me better, not bitter. That is one of the best decisions I could have made. We all have moments where a life circumstance can make us either bitter or better. Bitter does not wear well on one's face. Please let your circumstance become the grist in the mill. It may hurt now, but if you let the refiner's fire do its work, the craftsmanship of the true you will come out of that fire.

2. **What and WHO are you listening to? Protect your ear-gate at all costs and listen to the voices that will ONLY speak to your excellence.** My fiancé listened to the wrong voices (his single friends who spoke out of their own fear and of course the "other woman" who was speaking to him to entice him out of his covenant). At that critical juncture, I too, had to decide who to listen to. FAITH comes by hearing. *We always start believing the voices we listen to the most.* I was crushed. I was so emotionally devastated, looking back, I should have been under a doctor's care. But what I did have

was recordings of sermons, faith, business and motivational recordings. I knew if I played these 24/7, there would be healing in a deep level. I was wounded and this was a tool I could use. So I played these faith-filled motivational messages all the time. Day and night. My parents (who I had come to live with at this point) thought I had lost my mind. I was, in fact, using the motivation in those recordings to save myself. Remember much of our mainstream media and unfortunately many of our friends can be operating in fear without even realizing it. *What you listen to will penetrate your heart so be selective in media input, and any narrative from friends. Otherwise, you may become fearful and unable to conquer the obstacles ahead.*

3. **Just as a hunter is with a quiver of arrows, pulling one after another from quiver into the bow, you *must access your tools.* Use every single one.** I accessed my arrows. My friends (the ones who were deeply spiritual) could pray, stand with me and offer listening ears. Pain gets frozen when stuffed down. My faith in God had to be dusted off and truly strengthened. Spiritual wisdom became imperative. I studied ancient law, proverbs and scriptures on engagement, marriage and I most of all learned the power of love. The Bible tells us that love is stronger than the grave (Song of Solomon 8:6). This is true. I came to respect the powerful force of love. I came to understand the powerful force of words. "Death and life are in the fruit of the tongue" is a worthy proverb (Proverbs

18:21, ESV). I knew my words would arrive in my future ahead of me. As I undertook this journey, many things came to help me on my path. I even had dreams that would direct or show me what was to come! My spoken words of faith and what I listened to for healing made a big difference in my recovery.

4. **YOU are the deciding force.** When challenges come, you have a choice to fold or fight. If something is being taken from you—a job, a house, your health, a mate, just know, if you fold, your enemy wins and it is most likely gone for good. If you fight -- you have the shot at getting it back. It could be your health, your finances. Anything that is being wrongly taken. Stand in the gap for what you want. Pray, believe, speak it and ask others who have faith to stand with you. Do not just roll up when adversity hits. Stand against your challenge using the tools of faith, knowledge and the law. Do not be destroyed by a lack of knowledge. Know your rights in the universe, in scripture and in love. Love is a powerful force. Faith is a powerful force. Know what you want. Speak what you want. Decision is a powerful force.

5. **Find the specialist.** Believe me, there is always a person who has gone through what you are going through and has found victory on the other side. Find that expert. Follow them. Let them mentor you. They have walked that road and have come out victorious. Surprisingly, like a battle-worn soldier, most

of them, you will find, are more than happy to help you with their wisdom and tell you their war stories of how they fought. Yes, your journey may be slightly different but why reinvent the wheel? Listen to that specialist. Cut the learning curve. Take notes and follow their advice. Remember the adage: only take advice from those who have done what you want to do! There are a lot of "armchair critics". Take advice from those who were there before you and have come out victorious in the arena you are looking to conquer.

Yes, I was ill-prepared for this challenge. Yes, I was broken. I thought I would never smile again, laugh again, or smell again. I thought I had lost "me" forever. God did a miracle in my life. He picked up all those shattered pieces and put me back together again.

W.O.W. - Words of Wisdom

Change is hardest at the beginning, messiest in the middle, and gorgeous at the end.

— Robin Sharma

We are each here to impart our own unique gifting to the world. We each carry with us a puzzle piece necessary to complete this planet's picture. Your life is a mosaic. Some parts are messy on the backside while the surface is stunning. Some situations we cannot understand, yet later on in life they make sense and even become our strength. Please don't waste too much time looking back, trying to get even, wallowing in what-if's, when you can be putting energy into forward-moving creativity. Use every possible tool to get you through the tough times, and when the light comes on even if it's a flicker focus on creating something beautiful and new.

Marlena Martin is a native of San Diego and Graduate of the University of Southern California (USC) in Communication Theory. Marlena Martin is the Executive Director & Founder of Woman of Achievement, a National & International Recognition program for women making a difference in their communities. Marlena was a speaker at the Los Angeles March of Dimes, and participated in the *"Students Against Violence Program"* to bring awareness to bullying in schools, for which she received a Congressional commendation).

She was a recipient of the "Points of Light Presidential Community Service Award." Marlena was once a Legal Recruiter in Los Angeles, and was Sales Director with a major cosmetics company before developing womanofachievement.com.

She is a contributing author to two books chronicling the lives of various women founders, *"The She Shift,"* and *"It's All About Showing Up."*

RISE UP AND BUILD

By: Omenesa Oruma Akomolafe

After my scoliosis surgery, I rested for a couple of months. One fine morning, against my doctor's orders, I walked to school. Also, still hemorrhaging from a failed IVF for a twin pregnancy, I flew to a city called Aba to minister. The list of just how many times I had felt knocked to the ground, yet got up undeterred, is endless. *Rising up* and dusting my pants is something I seem to have mastered so well. While I can't remember a time when I didn't or couldn't rise up again, I can certainly recall instances in which I didn't and couldn't rise up *immediately*. Indeed, the real conflict is battling with the consequences of not rising up at all, especially when the burden of life weighs so heavily on our frail shoulders, and we are caught in the valley between the mountains of *Giving Up* and *Rising Up*. You can take a little breather on the floor if you wish. Yet, you must *rise up*.

I will now relate how 2017 became a turning point in my life. In 2007, I *rose up* and left Dallas, Texas, where I'd attended college for many years. Despite an initial plan to move to Detroit, I ended up in Kentucky, where my mom and I became flat mates. Apart from being a bishop's wife, my mom was a home healthcare aide (HHA). One day, despite having worked mostly in retail, a desire came upon me to care for the sick without necessarily becoming a doctor. My mom introduced me to her agency, and I *rose up* to start my new job as a HHA.

My first patient had cancer. At night, I'd hear voices surrounding my patient, but as soon I got close, they stopped. It was all very strange to me. I worked the 7pm to 7am shift. One day, her family called me. She was lying comatose in the living room. A catholic priest was reciting the final rites. She died that night. I was asked by her family to sing at her funeral. I felt honored. That was when I knew I was gifted in providing bereavement services and would probably do more so in the future. I continued to pick up shifts until I got married in 2011, and *rose up* to Nigeria to return to the entertainment business.

Then came 2017. My mom announced that she had cancer. This was a formal announcement since she had known for quite some time that she was sick, but didn't tell me or my dad. She was a reverend and was known to pray for the sick and they recovered, so I eventually understood why she might have felt embarrassed, angry and frustrated. When I found out about her cancer, I told her I would take care of her. I had just finished my first round of IVF, and lost the two embryos. So it was actually in absolute agony that I made her that promise. She probably didn't believe me because of my own condition. Besides, she was already on her way to America for treatment, and she didn't see me picking myself up to take care of her. Her thinking was wrong. She started radiation treatment in America, while I stayed back to do another round of IVF, this time for a triplet pregnancy. Two weeks after the procedure, I *rose up* and flew to Maryland to take care of my mom. I was expecting my triplets, in the hope that they had been successfully implanted by the IVF. I walked into the room. My mom was stunned. "Ah you came. You came."

All her hair was gone. I had dreamt about her before my trip. She looked exactly as she did in the dream, so I wasn't exactly shocked. I repeated what I told her in my dream. "You are so beautiful." Immediately, I began my assignment, my ministry as her personal HHA/CNA. Everything now made sense. I now knew why God had groomed me in that position years ago. I witnessed her screams of pain at night. Sometimes, I would be in the shower or in the kitchen, and would hear her scream my name. I would run out quickly, only to find her sleeping. Her constant pain had become a part of me, for I now heard her even when she wasn't speaking. I remembered my first encounter as an HHA, and it all suddenly made sense, as my mother too was talking to dead people, including her father that only she could see.

I read the bible to her. I sang to her. I prayed with her. I listened to music with her. I wrote in my journal daily, taking notes of all she said to me. I penned down all her prayers. She would tell me not to worry, as I would be relieved soon. She never mentioned that she would die, but she alluded to it. My father and I were bewildered by the entire experience, but we were thankful to be there for her. Dad did the cooking, while I did the ADL. We were hosted by my parents' mentees of over 30 years. We were like family. My dad bought her a night gown every day. She went to bed wearing a new nightgown daily. That was his way of coping. They had been married for 44 years.

The day came when she was no longer speaking. A rattle was in her throat. She could no longer eat. She refused medication. I frantically crushed her Tramadol, while dad grinded her food to a puree consistency. The day came when she could no longer bear weight as I tried to transfer her from her couch to her wheelchair. We both went down slowly to the ground. She looked at me and said, "I am going to meet my Maker." A few days later, we took her to the hospital. Her organs were already failing. I was not ready. I just wasn't ready. She and I had barely got along for so many years, and I wanted to savor the moment God had so graciously restored to us. She apologized and so did I. Six weeks of a brand new relationship was built, and I absolutely fell in love with this woman who I saw as God's child, and not as a titled woman; Mother, Mommie, First Lady, Bishop's Wife, Women's Leader.

One evening, her threshold for pain was broken, and as everyone ran around frantically seeking a suitable drug to give her, Mom and I looked at each other for the last time. Our eyes locked. We both knew the inevitable was about to occur. Twelve hours later, my friend was gone. My mother died. All I had left with me was the green diary in which I wrote daily, and ruminations of her voice when she would scream my name, "Meme, pain. Pain." That was her way of telling me she needed Tramadol. Meme was the pet name she had called me for 34 years.

I was filled with guilt because I left to go to the hospital chapel, and she died in my absence. It hurt me to my marrow because many times, she had begged me not to leave her. I still haven't forgiven myself to this day. As I crawled on that hospital floor like a spider screaming, "I left her," the nurses reminded me that I had not showered nor left the hospital in days. In fact, there was a comb permanently stuck in my hair. I had been unkempt for almost a week. I was frazzled and throwing up the day before she died. I was asked to choose a funeral home the day before her death, and with a heavy heart, I had one in mind.

I held it together. I looked strong. My father, while walking down the hospital hall, would see me and say, "You are so strong!" I did not consider it a compliment. It was not strength. It was agony for which I couldn't find expression. I eventually broke into pieces weeks after she passed. It took me two years to recover from the severe panic attacks that started as soon as she died.

Nevertheless, I forged ahead. I *rose up*. After burying her, I left my very public life. I left the honorariums and the Lady O brand. I left the microphone and I *rose up*. I moved to New York to become a nurse. My husband and father thought I was crazy, especially since I lost the supposed triplets a few days after arriving in Maryland. Everyone thought I would try again as compensation for my multiple losses. Instead, I channeled all my energy into becoming a certified home healthcare aide.

My first patient in New York was a cancer patient. He too was in hospice. Every gap I left unfilled with my mother, I filled with his life. I never left his side. Then, I became a CNA, and ended up taking care of seven to twenty hospice patients every night. Shortly after, Covid-19 hit, and my landlord died. I ended up homeless. I slept at the church, and sometimes on the floor. One day, after praying and groaning for two weeks, I got three jobs. I *rose up*, and began working 60 to 86-hour shifts. I ended up bagging dead patients, and still did most nights, as most of my patients were geriatrics and hospice residents. I became a CPE student in a Hospice Hospital in New York, and I enrolled into an LPN program, so that I could comfortably man my hospice and bereavement agency, which I founded after my mom died. It is called 'Angels on Duty.' We are mostly *Death Doulas,* but bridge the gap so well, as we write letters to loved ones, bathe and massage the patient and plan the funeral. This is the ministry that was birthed by my mother's demise.

Leaving a legacy has become my mantra and mandate. I *rose up* two months after losing my apartment, and finally got my own two-bedroom apartment. I was now settled as a New Yorker. I was able to fully return to my entertainment life, and I now run a ministry, my music career and hospice care concurrently. I was able to write an over 600-page book about my grieving process titled, "A

Selfish Turn." I am now my Dad's sole caregiver. He misses Mom so much. His life is a gift I beg God not to take away anytime soon.

When life knocks you down, you'll be presented with a decision. Are you going to stay down, or will you rise up? I kept getting up because I was able to see the bigger picture. *What do you see ahead of you?* If you can't see that big picture, it might be hard for you to get up. The picture is your candy, an incentive to get up. There is something out there written with your name on it. You have to get up to grab it. While still believing God to give me children, I know that my heir is not my legacy. My legacy is my heir. Therefore I work hard daily to build my business, ministry and agencies, and I have them all set up so that they can be carried over to the next generation.

Use your experiences to build your legacy. Use infertility to open support groups. Use abuse to start seminars. Use homelessness to open shelters. Use single-handedness to teach self-love. When you face loss, cry your eyes out. Allow yourself to feel the sting, and then breathe. Mourn until your loss loses its pang. Then build on all you've learned. Remember that there is a win in every loss. Continue to *RISE UP*.

W.O.W. - Words of Wisdom

Out of the huts of history's shame, I rise. Up from a past that's rooted in pain, I rise.

- Maya Angelou

Know that the human spirit is indomitable. Although life's trials can be heart wrenching, sometimes causing you to crumble to your knees in agony and distress, the spirit can still rise from the depths to the top. Let that truth be the hope at the end of the tunnels in which you find yourself. Rising up is an ability embedded deep inside of you. Tap into your greatness and power.

Omenesa Akomolafe is a Preacher, Pastor, Prison Chaplain, Music Minister, Writer, TV Show Host, Certified Life Coach, Certified Confidence Coach, Emotional Healing Practitioner, Emotional Nudist and a Certified Nursing Assistant. She has found enduring passion in healing the Emotionally Broken, and has been a veritable conduit for emotional transformation in the lives of many. With a concentration on anointed music, the word and impartation, Omenesa's aim is to heal what's wounded in the pews, and coaches Church Choirs.

She writes for reputable Pastors, and businesspersons on the platform of her Publishing Company, Pencil's Corner. Omenesa has a Diploma in Child Psychology, Bachelors in Church Ministries, and Certification as a Home Health Aide.

She is currently working on an Advanced Diploma in Thanatology, and doing a combined B.A, M.A and Ph.D. in Metaphysics. She is married to Omoniyi Joseph Akomolafe, a Pastor, Cinematographer, Worship Minister, and Entrepreneur.

Lead Yourself First

By: Di Carter

"Ask, Seek and Knock"

* * *

God is the ultimate leader, and He does so with grace and patience. He has equipped us from birth to listen and follow in faith. The problem is we don't always listen to and trust His plan. Once you start listening to God, you can feel the Spirit speaking to you so loudly that it is impossible to ignore. You may not understand His plan and feel that it is menial, but it may impact others in a way that will change their lives.

When God called me to be a leader of my first business, I was almost paralyzed with fear. *Am I equipped? Am I enough?* I thought. *Am I ready? What if I do not have the grit, discipline or knowledge to do it? Worst of all: What if I let my future employees down, those that would trust me enough to choose to work for my company?*

The fear of the unknown will keep you small, but worship, prayers and positive motivation will take away that fear, and will allow those around you to recognize you as a leader that they want to follow. This earns you the "Lead by example" badge.

I am a mom of twins and a social entrepreneur. I have been working as a professional network marketer for over four years. In all honesty, I had become frustrated because I was unable to grow

s, and I knew I needed a big change in my network
or risk quitting the industry altogether. I knew I
o I began to pray and ask fearlessly for a new
from home.

lunch with Robbie Motter, Shelly Ruffin and
no on the Queen Mary in California, I
y approach to social media as it related to my
m my personal mentor, Robbie Motter, the
vhat you want and being very specific. She
The power is in the asking." And so I began asking.

I grew my first online business from $0 to $5k a month in only six short months. The goal now is $10k in less than one year. How did I do it? By leading myself first.

The power of asking is the first step of leading yourself. You must humble yourself and face the reality of your failure or unhappiness with the situation that you are currently in. You have to ask God for direction and be open to receive instructions, regardless of how difficult it may seem. I needed to grow in a way that I have not grown before.

In February 2020, I prayed to God for a new top leader in Network Marketing to help guide me out of this rut I was in:

Dear Heavenly Father, I pray that this new vision you are downloading in my mind will glorify YOU. Lord, you know my heart. Help me decide whether to change companies or not. Help my transition to be smooth. Please bless the ones who are not coming with me. Lord, I ask YOU to guide me to someone who will push me beyond my limits. A leader who will understand my lifestyle, who is loving toward me and my future team. Lord, I ask for a new place full of joy, celebration, and an atmosphere that feels like home to all. Help us impact the world in YOUR name. In Jesus' Name, Amen.

Nine months went by, and I still had no answer. Meanwhile, I was growing my team and getting close to hitting $200k in volume sales. Out of what felt like nowhere, I frequently started seeing the numbers 7, double 77 and triple 777. People would message me with quotes about positive changes, and one of my friends, Natasha, revealed that big changes were about to happen.

Everything I have been praying for showed up in front of me via Facebook Live. The leaders I dreamt of, were right in front of me. I watched The Zolecki's from afar on social media, and, without hesitating, started a beautiful friendship, first with Sarah Zolecki and later Tony, her husband. She was a mom of two kids just like me. She was spontaneous, fun, loving and, most importantly, she smiled all the time like I do.

The courageous act of asking through prayers for a new opportunity, being patient and waiting for God's timing was crucial. I could have quit network marketing altogether and never discovered the amazing opportunity of being where I am and building the team that I have today. I was seeking a change, and with that came the consequences. I had to say goodbye to my sponsor, team and the company that I was in love with for 3.5 years. I cried; my team cried. They did not want to come with me, and I respected their decision.

What I did find was a dream team, top leaders, and products that I adore. I have never felt so welcomed on a team. I was very sure that I was going to use all my gifts within the new opportunity.

We all hit the ground running, day one. We all decided to go hard, or go home. I looked at my mentors and said, "Its show time!" My first customer was a very close friend, Tina. She prayed and loved me and, because of her words, I knew I would be okay.

Seek, and you shall find, and I started my first 30-day run. I had my eyes on the prize, and I knew I wanted to break records every 30 days. I set my goal on what I could control, and I became master of my emotions. *Celebrate every no with a happy smile,* I told myself and it was the best thing I could do.

The (MMA) money-making activities in Network Marketing are prospecting, following up and adding new friends, building your list daily and promoting events to your team. Although I couldn't control the outcomes, I could control my daily actions because my habits determined my success. It was not simple to *ask* daily, but the results made me feel amazing.

397 Invitations, 263 Follow ups, 78 newly added friends in 30 days. The Results: 7 promotions, and I won a company prize, a Fitbit Versa that I gifted to my husband on Christmas. He loved it!

Anyone at any point in their life can start from 0 every 30 days and succeed if they are intentional.

After those 30 days, it was my job to keep leading me, showing up and being the leader, I wanted to have. It is true! When the student is ready, the teacher will show up. I kept doing whatever my leaders asked me to do. Trust me, 80% of the time, I was uncomfortable, but I did it anyway. I noticed that every 30 days, I was growing my confidence level, and I could not stop being grateful for my team, the company and the leaders with whom God surrounded me.

The gates have been opened, and the business is now overflowing with love, recognition and appreciation for what we do daily to change thousands of lives. Yes, I am making $5K a month, and I am on my way to doubling that, but it has never been about the money. It is truly about seeing people discover themselves through your example to show up and lead with passion. To see them spread their wings and win like they never won before.

Remember God is the ultimate leader, and He calls for you to lead with grace. He will qualify the unqualified and all you need to do is step in faith and lead yourself first.

W.O.W. - Words of Wisdom

Ask, and it shall be given you. Seek, and you shall find. Knock, and it will be opened to you.

- Matthew 7:7, NIV

Don't stop asking, seeking and knocking because the power is in the asking! Step out in bold faith, set audacious goals and be your own best competition.

Di Carter is an immigrant from Brazil, who is the founder of No-Profit Christfest PC 503c, CEO of a successful international distribution center, Mrs. Indiana woman of achievement 2021, and network marketing top Leader in health & wellness. She is also a #1 International Bestseller who is very passionate about online home-based business, recruiting, and community service.

Recently, Di started coaching mom's on their journey to quit smoking, and find their journey to live longer, happier and healthier. She believes "you are made for more." and God has given you a gift to bless others with.

When Di isn't running her businesses, she spends quality time with her husband, two beautiful twin girls, and helps the less fortunate through global mission trips.

Helping Women Soar to Greatness: There's Power In the Asking

By: Robbie Motter

* * *

There is a well-known saying: *Closed mouths don't get fed.* Of this, I am a firm believer. I had been blessed to be an integral part of The National Association for Female Entrepreneurs as Global Coordinator for 29 years before forming The Global Society for Female Entrepreneurs (GSFE) in 2017. From a young age, I have always declared that whatever my lot, I could be the change that I wanted to see in the earth. It is that principle that has gifted me with the opportunity to empower over 10,000 women through my organizations to soar into their entrepreneurial greatness. Many would not believe that I have had to overcome the stigmas and obstacles of foster care in my formative years; most times being the only one in my circle that encouraged myself to believe that I was made for greatness.

I guess I have always been a trailblazer, unbeknownst to myself as a young woman. Even as a youth in the foster care system, I would encourage others to take charge of their destiny; after all, they were capable of greater things. I would tell them. "Take one day at a time and do not let anyone destroy your dreams and goals." In grade school, I played intramural basketball, where I was able to hone my love of teamwork and motivation. As a student leader, I worked with my team's coaches to discover innovative ways to allow us to play more games. This drive to motivate continued in my career aspirations, as I started employment at the ripe age of fourteen years old. Even in that entry level position, I spent a good amount of leisure time studying how I could advance in business, keeping my eyes on promotion. I learned how to work hard at whatever I did, and developed a strong work ethic. Still, while being very goal-oriented, I recognized the importance of connection.

I always took time to listen to my coworkers. If I knew someone that could help another person, I would connect them. I always believed that although society as a whole seemed to be in constant competition, we could do more together by efficiently working together. Not everyone believed in the power of collaboration. At one of my earliest office jobs in Omaha, Nebraska, I remember asking an older woman to teach me how to do a particular task that was needed for a project. After looking me up and down, she dismissed me almost immediately. "I will not teach you, or any woman," she said, leaving me flabbergasted as she strolled back to her cubicle. From that day on, I made it my passion to share with women whatever I learned. I didn't let that incident or any other discouragement for that matter, deter me from attaining the skills I needed to advance my career. But it did make me doubt asking anyone to help me when I was in need, for fear of rejection and disappointment. As a helper and encourager at heart, I sometimes struggled with asking for or accepting help from others.

One day, a colleague said to me, "Robbie, you get such pleasure in helping others, don't you?" "Yes, it fills my heart and soul," I responded. "Well, why don't you let us have that same pleasure of helping you?" That really made me think; from then on, it became easier to ASK. Eventually, my confidence and tenacity grew and I became known for never taking *NO* for an answer. A *NO* from one just meant, ASK *someone else*. Sometimes, gathering the courage to ask for assistance was an obstacle in itself, especially on the heels of a previous rejection. Nevertheless, I learned to let my love for helping others outweigh the fear of *NO*. I've learned that our *NO's* challenge us to overcome rejection, think outside of the box for solutions and refocus our energy on the goal. In the *NO* moments, we must ask ourselves: "What is our highest priority what will it accomplish, and will it touch a life or make a difference?" If our need qualifies as one of those highest priorities, then we must forge ahead unafraid and show up regardless. The POWER is in the Asking.

Showing up, to me, is like receiving a treasure map for a buried mystery. But if you follow through after showing up, you will find the treasure within. On January 22, 2021 I co-authored a book called ***It's All About Showing Up the Power is in the Asking*** with 46 collaborators. The coauthors were all GSFE members who shared their SHOW UP and ASK stories. For 90% of the coauthors, it was their first time collaborating on a book or writing a story. Those women stepped out of their comfort zone and did it! On the day of our launch, we made #1 U.S. Bestseller on Amazon and Barnes & Noble, and then the next day made #1 International Bestseller. The book is now available on all major platforms. Several of the coauthors have since gone on to write their own books. However, it was *our* project that served as the catalyst to know they could do it, and they did. To this day, we still get numerous emails telling us how the book has inspired or changed lives.

At 85 years old, I can look back at my life with a sense of pride and look to the future with a sense of excitement. My passion until my last breath will be to support women, to inspire them and let them know they are not alone; to help them see that they can achieve whatever their dream without letting anyone or anything stand in their way. Nothing is impossible.

W.O.W. - Words of Wisdom

For it was I, the LORD your God, who rescued you from the land of Egypt. Open your mouth wide, and I will fill it with good things.

- **Psalm 81:10, NLT**

God Himself encourages us to open our mouths wide, so that He can fill it with good things. This should give us the confidence we need to transform the fear of asking into an expectation of joy!

Robbie Motter is Founder of Global Society for Female Entrepreneurs (GSFE), a nonprofit, and an International Best Selling Author of two books, "It's All About Showing Up," and the "POWER is in the ASKING." She is Mentor, Business Coach, Marketing/PR Consultant, Certified National Speaker, Author, Radio Show Host, Writer, and Advisory Board Member of "SIMA (She Inspires Me).

She is focused on empowering, mentoring, inspiring and educating women so they can become successful entrepreneurs.

globalsocietyforfemaleentreprenuers.org

www.robbiemotter.com

WHAT'S IN YOUR DASH?

By: Kenise A. Etwaru

* * *

I am sure you have been to a cemetery and have seen a tombstone. Typically on a tombstone, you'll find the name of the person, a little blurb and then some dates. The dates represent the year the person was born and the year the person died. In the middle of the date is a symbol called a "dash" (-). It's pretty insignificant because no one ever focuses on the dash. Who takes a second look at the dash? No one, it's just there.

In this chapter, I will be focusing on the meaning and the purpose that dash has in our lives by telling you my story. I do not want to sound morbid, but when the time comes for the Lord to call me home, my dash will have a lot of trials that become triumphant testimonies.

I was raised in a Godly home, where both of my parents are Pastors. I have been attending church since I was in my mother's womb, which is a very long time. I know everything about church because I have spent most of my time hanging out there. Of course, because I spent so much time there, I was really involved in many different areas within the church.

One of the key areas I have been involved in is praise and worship. At the age of 16, I became the worship leader in my local church. There I was, the youngest person on the worship team and they made me the worship leader. "Kenise, lead everyone into worship" were all the words I heard over and over again. I took those words to heart and focused my heart and mind on fulfilling the purpose God had for me. Little did I know that walking on purpose was not all sunshine, rainbows and flowers. No one warned me of what was to come.

I was so focused on God and working in my local church, I really did not date much. I focused heavily on my ministry and of course, finishing school and my career. I worked on completing my undergraduate degree in business in three years, instead of four and then moved on to getting my graduate degree. By the time I completed my undergraduate degree, I got the job of my dreams in Manhattan and my career began booming.

Due to the fact that I never really dated, the time just flew by and I was now in my late twenties. I really did not think about the man I wanted to marry, but I figured now was a good time to get married. About a year later, there was the man of dreams. He was an amazing musician, which was a strong commonality we both shared. He was also a PK (Pastor's Kid) just like me. He was a bit unstable with his walk with God, but he said he was working on it. After a year of dating, we began talking about marriage. Even though my parents were reluctant due to his past, because he was married before and had a daughter, plus his walk with God was not always consistent, I prayed and knew that this was the man God had for me. After dating for a year, he proposed and we courted for another year while planning our dream wedding.

YAY!! My dream wedding! June 24th, 2007 was set as THE DATE to be one of the greatest days of my life. I articulately planned every single detail of my wedding day, which included over 500 guests, a butterfly release, trumpeters, food galore, breathtaking flowers, beautiful outfits, the perfect venue on Long Island and so much more. Hands down, I had the most amazing wedding day a girl could ask for. Life as I know it was just beautiful.

After getting married, we decided to enjoy being newlyweds and waited to have children. After waiting three years, in January 2010, our daughter, Aviah was born. Before our daughter arrived, we travelled and spent a lot of time working at our local church. It was just great! Everyone repeatedly told us that we were the perfect couple and I was not going to disagree.

In August of 2010, my husband and I agreed that I would take a girls' vacation and he would go on vacation with his sister and brother-in-law. It is just incredible to know how your life can change in one week. That week-long vacation changed the trajectory of our marriage. When he returned from vacation, I felt like something just was not right. He looked and acted very differently. There was a disconnect. A few weeks after he returned, as we were driving together one morning, I saw a glimpse of his cell phone and there was a text message that said, *"Miss you babe"*. I asked him who sent that text and he said, "You did." Really? How and why would I send him a text (1) while I am driving and (2) why would I tell him that I miss you when we are both sitting in the same car driving for over an hour. That was the beginning of the worst time of my life. The lies and more lies piled on. To this day, I still have not been told the truth as to who that person was or why she was texting him. We ended up separating for about a month and he begged me to come back. I prayed on it and as I looked at my one and half year old baby girl, I thought about the questions she would have for me later in life. We got back together with hopes of working on our marriage and figuring out what happened. Of course, he did not want to go to counseling because he said that it was not necessary. I would ask him the question almost daily, "What did I do wrong?"

The Easter weekend, just five months after we got back together, he came to me and said that he wanted to go back to Guyana on vacation. So, I told him that would be fine with me. We would all go as a family. Nope, that was not what he wanted. He said he just needed a break and some time off and when he returned, we would continue to work on our marriage. I cannot even explain the pain and the nauseating feeling in the pit of my stomach. Why did he want to go back? What was in Guyana that I could not give to him? The questions became too much. I went to the Lord again. I poured out my heart and cried asking Him to show me what I needed to do. I felt the peace of God in that room in the midst of my mixed up emotions, tears, pain and agony. The Lord showed up and told me that He was in control. The next day, I sat on the couch next to my husband and asked him to please tell me what I did wrong. He could not look at me in my eyes. It had been months since he looked me in the eyes. However, after many months, he looked at me directly in my eyes and said, "Kenise, it's not you, it's me. Something is wrong with me".

WOW! The relief that I felt at that moment knowing that I toiled for months and months, beating myself up because I felt I did something wrong and just could not figure out what I did to lose my husband. He continued to tell me that he did not want the marriage because he was in love with someone else. He said he still had feelings for me and wanted to be with me but he needed some time. In that moment, in the midst of those painful words from the man I was in love with, the Fathers' love (simply indescribably) overshadowed me. I released my husband. He left a few days later to go back to Guyana and told me that he would work on the marriage when he returned. My last words to him when he called me as he was boarding the plane were: "If you are on the plane when the tires take off from the tarmac, this marriage is over". He left me. At that moment in time, I began creating my own dash. Now, nine years later since my divorce, I look back and reflect. If it was not for that situation, I would not be the woman leaving a legacy today.

I have learned that there are two specific areas that will change your perspective of the dash and how it relates to your life. How can your dash have meaning? What kind of significance will your dash have on your life and you leaving a legacy? Let me tell you something, I'm all about how loaded my dash will be when it's written on my tombstone. People will look at my dash and it will actually speak of my life, purpose and legacy, and each one of them will be fulfilled according to God's ultimate plan and purpose.

1. IDENTITY:

First and foremost, let's begin with knowing who we are and knowing our identity. Did you know that God has created YOU in His image? If you do not know where you come from, then you cannot know where you are destined to go. You will be like a nomad wandering around life. It is sad because in the world today, many people, including believers, do not know where they came from and thereby struggle with their identity. They simply don't know who they are. Allow me to inform you, if this is your first time hearing this or remind you if you have forgotten, who you are:

- Created in the image of God
- Formed according to the likeness of God
- Fearfully and wonderfully made
- Intricately and delicately designed by the Creator who formed you in your mother's womb

2. PURPOSE:

Once you know your identity, it becomes easier to understand your purpose and then live with a passion and desire to fulfill it. Let me now introduce to or remind you of the purpose God has for your life.

- Jeremiah 29:11 (NIV) - *'For I know the plans I have for you,' declares the Lord, 'plans to prosper you and not to harm you, plans to give you hope and a future.'*
- 1 Peter 2:9 (NIV)- *But you are a chosen race, a royal priesthood, a holy nation, a people for his own possession, that you may proclaim the excellencies of him who called you out of darkness into his marvelous light.*
- Ephesians 1:5 (NIV) - *He predestined us for adoption as sons through Jesus Christ, according to the purpose of his will.*
- Exodus 9:16 (NIV) - *But I have raised you up for this very purpose, that I might show you my power and that my name might be proclaimed to all the earth.*

The scripture verses mentioned are just a reminder of how much God desires us to live a life of purpose. God's ultimate agenda once we know who we are, is to help us live a life committed and passionate about fulfilling the purposes of God; then, and only then, will we be able to create and fulfill our legacy.

W.O.W. - Words of Wisdom

Be very careful, then, how you live—not as unwise but as wise, making the most of every opportunity,

- Ephesians 5:15-16a, NIV

Redeem the time while you still have life. Tomorrow is not promised! Dwell on the impact you want to make before you leave this earth, and begin to make steps towards that vision of impact from there. Make the most of every opportunity (YES! Every opportunity...the good, the bad and the ugly) in wisdom, and allow God to partner with you, thereby making you unstoppable.

Kenise Etwaru educational background is in Human Resources. She has built HR departments for major private and non-profit organizations in New York City.

Kenise is also a songwriter, musician, recording artist, executive leadership coach, women empowerment strategist, 4x bestselling author, international motivational speaker and entrepreneur/CEO.

She also runs a daily Facebook LIVE devotional to help encourage believers and non-believers to Read the Word, Pray the Word, Write the Word and Apply the Word.

She resides on Long Island, New York, where she is the Music Minister and a Board Member at her parents' church in Richmond Hill, Queens.

www.KeniseEtwaru.com | www.aleapublishingllc.com | Facebook: @Kenise Etwaru | Instagram: @kenise_etwaru | LinkedIn: @Kenise Etwaru

LEAD BY FAITH OVER FEAR

Taking a Leap of Faith!

Dedicated to the women who choose to lead by faith over fear.

By: Tracea Bolin

* * *

After graduating high school, I decided to take a leap of faith and join the United States Navy. I joined undesignated, a decision no one makes because it means the Navy can assign you anywhere they want. I was determined and ready to launch, so I trusted God as I led myself forward in faith. I was glad they gave each of us a mini New Testament Bible, as I was walking by faith during this time. It was a struggle to endure the many phases and tests I endured through boot camp and I would read God's Word in that little Bible to stand on His truth in faith. I was selected for the drill team there and later served as a USN Ceremonial Guard in Washington DC. As a proven female leader in my service, I was then offered to serve as a personal secretary for Naval Bupers at the Pentagon. What an incredible journey my faith had taken me on in the first couple of years—and I had only just begun! I was then offered by the Admiral to attend the Naval and Marine Intelligence School so I could advance in a job designation of my choice. I had to have faith again, as I was being sent across the country by myself. After graduating, I was assigned to the VP47 Squadron based in California, served on Diego Garcia, and eventually transferred to Hawaii.

In Hawaii, I continued the passion I had possessed for pageantry since a young age. This also bought me a new sense of confidence in my faith to overcome my fear and lead many other women by example. I entered many local competitions and won Miss Oahu International 1994 and Miss Island Ilima 1995. I competed for Miss Hawaii America 1995, a preliminary for Miss America.

After my obligated service to my country was complete, I decided to come back to the States and see my family, and this is around the time that I met my husband. Taking yet another leap of faith, we got engaged within three months of meeting and married six months after. We have been married for 25 years now. To God be the Glory!

But without faith it is impossible to [walk with God and] please Him, for whoever comes [near] to God must [necessarily] believe that God exists and that He rewards hose who [earnestly and diligently] seek Him.

–   Hebrews 11:6 AMP

How Much Can You Take and Overcome? About twelve years ago, I was diagnosed with rheumatoid arthritis. It all happened gradually as I started feeling pain and weakness in my legs and hands. As the arthritis progressed, I had to have a hip replacement, two knee replacements and a metal plate put in my wrist. I also had skin issues that would not heal. This is when I would stand on His promises—not on what was actually going on, but on God's Word of truth.

Faith shows the reality of what we hope for; it is the evidence of things we cannot see.

− Hebrews 11:1 NLT

I decided to follow this advice. My faith led me straight to doctors who placed me on the right medications to bring healing to my body. The inflammation has subsided, and the wounds are closed. To God be the Glory! He used this trial to help others, as they have seen me overcome such adversity.

I chose to lead by faith through my trials. I led by becoming an advocate of the Arthritis Foundation and a captain for The Cure for Arthritis Walk held every year to raise awareness of arthritis. In all of this, I have been a light of hope and encouragement to many by showing what I have overcome.

No One Can Take You Out Before Your Time! Fear tactics have long been one of the enemy's most effective weapons that he tries to use against us. The Bible instructs us to not be afraid. We must replace our fear with faith. As a mighty woman of faith, I was once in a situation where a gunman opened fire from the parking lot into the store I was in, shattering the glass through my vehicle parked in front of the store. As I darted in the office for cover with an employee, we sat on the floor not knowing what was next. I thought, *Lord, I have no protection if the gunman comes in here.* The Lord spoke to me saying, *Yes, you do! You know my Word!* Fear tried to grip me, but faith rose up and I declared the Word of truth in the situation. I shouted, "No weapon formed against us shall prosper in Jesus' name!" At that moment, things seemed to settle down and we were able to come out. The shooter fled the scene, and when I looked at my car, it was the only one shot up, totaled and riddled with bullets. The enemy had to flee in Jesus' name! By the Word of God, we put things into motion. I truly believe no one can take you out before your time or before your destiny is fulfilled. We must lead our lives with the Word of God.

You see, all of us experience fear at different points in our lives. We have to choose faith over fear—they cannot both rule at the same time. We must choose which one we will embrace, and which we will abandon. I have learned through my experiences that what we do with our fear is what determines how we allow ourselves to experience life. Fear is what ultimately holds many women leaders back from experiencing success. God's purpose for me is to love and serve others, and bring glory to Him. I have had times where I've had to surrender my will, emotions and heart to God in order to lead.

I believe I have been given this time here on earth to fulfill my God-given destiny and purpose. Finish the race; fight the good fight of faith. If I ever doubt how far I can go, I can always remember how far I have come already. My goodness, that alone is a grand testimony itself! I have been given this life because I am strong enough to live it to the fullest.

W.O.W. - Words of Wisdom

And one day she discovered that she was fierce, and strong, and full of fire, and that not even she could hold herself back because her passion burned brighter than her fears.

— Mark Anthony

Father God, I pray that we can find true meaning, purpose and hope in our lives. We can rise up to lead with purpose and vision, with Faith over Fear. Give us strength and the heart of a warrior to press through everything YOU have in store for us. Let us trust in YOUR perfect plan and let Your Word transform our hearts. Amen.

Trachea Bolin is Mrs. Universe Tourism 2021, and works at East Coast Perfect Woman Supermodel 2021 and Worlds Perfect East Coast Modeling and Pageant Championship. She is also America Ambassador at International Face Magazine.

She is a past Woman of Achievement, and Mrs. Mid Atlantic United States 2018.

www.facebook.com/tracea.bolin/

Beauty for Ashes

By: Tracy Shy Simmons

* * *

I spent a decade of my life with my eyes firmly closed. My life was quickly going downhill, but I refused to see it. I was in denial, unwilling and unable to see how poor choices had left me weary and downtrodden. I had been blessed with an ability to bless others through my God-given voice, but I was blinded by my own shame and regret. Truthfully, I was spiritually dying. However, God was not going to allow that to happen, and He opened my eyes to the truth I had been denying.

This story begins one night in Philadelphia. I had been invited to attend an exclusive conference for significant figures of the gospel music industry: recording artists, agents and studio executives. My friends and I attended together, excited to make connections with others who shared our mission: using our music to worship God. At the conference, I was very impressed by one particular musician, who displayed such remarkable talent that I felt I needed to share my appreciation. When we spoke, I was struck by his charm and confidence. When he asked me on a date that very night, I was excited to agree. One date led to another and another and another, and soon I found myself falling in love with this man. My world revolved around him, and I knew I wanted to spend my life with him. We soon moved in together, which was new and strange to me, but I knew that we would get married no matter what.

But our life together was not as perfect as it seemed. He was lying to me constantly, but I closed my eyes to it. I remember one Sunday, we attended church together, and after I'd left my purse with him for a few minutes, I soon noticed that money was missing. I should have confronted him about it, but instead, I chose to ignore it and went ahead with the wedding.

Even at the time, I knew I should not have married him; in fact, I told my mother on my wedding day that God had told me not to go through with it. But I did anyway, and I paid dearly for it. I remember many of the devastating situations he put me in, leaving me embarrassed and ashamed. He left me waiting in the car for him for hours after taking my money and never returned. He went back to homes we visited and would steal all of the valuables. He sold fake drugs to a woman who showed up at my door with a baseball bat, ready to swing. He collected money from my friends and music group to buy a birthday gift for me, but instead pocketed the money. Over and over and over again, something terrible would happen, and I would ask him to tell me what was going on, only to be answered with an endless cycle of excuses for his behavior. And I ate every single excuse up. Like most women, I wanted to *fix it* for him, but I didn't realize that I myself needed to be *fixed* before I could truly help. And only God could fix me.

I was at my lowest, but I kept holding on to this relationship. I was told to stay, I was told to pray, I was told to believe in him, but I could feel part of me dying each day as I was ground into the dust. Every highlight of my life was a trigger for his binges, leaving me to pick up the pieces afterwards, unable to understand why my life had reached this point. Feeling responsible for his behavior, I tried to repay the people he harmed, but a friend told me that I needed to stop trying to atone for something I didn't do. Even my mother told me one day, "Tracy, you don't love yourself." I couldn't understand what they were saying until I had a sudden epiphany.

One day as I was praying, I came to a realization: God wasn't moving in my life. My life was not getting any better by holding on, so maybe I needed to try moving. I needed to reevaluate God's place in my life and my priorities. I recognized that God had always protected me and blessed me. He opened many doors for me in the music industry and kept me safe in all walks of life. As I communed with God, I could feel an overwhelming feeling in my soul, a message from God, saying, *Come on, I got something for you to do. You're still valuable. I still love you. I still need you. I will always be here.* That realization transformed me, because though this marriage held only false fulfillment for me, it had truly brought me closer to my savior and my deliverer.

From that moment on, I set out to relate to God one-on-one, building a personal relationship with the God who had always helped me to do what I needed to do. He opened my eyes to the truth of who I was. I had never liked looking at myself in the mirror. I would mainly use it to check my makeup or quickly glance at my outfit, but God taught me how to truly see myself, and like who I saw. My past experiences did not need to define me; the only thing that would define me was my relationship with God. I had spent years living a lie, dying a little every day, losing that potential for service and ministering God has cultivated within me. I lost sight of the joy and beauty of communing with God and allowing Him into my life, but now that I have rediscovered it, it has brought me to new heights of existence, pushing me to be the best Tracy I could possibly be.

Even in the midst of my struggles, I always knew God worked miracles in my life. Looking back at some of the experiences I have had, I can see how everything I had been through was a making and breaking experience for me, pushing me to rely on Him in every thought and every action. My disobedience had made my life hard, and my shame had kept me from going to God for deliverance. At the heart of me, I knew that God was my shepherd, and He would always take care of me. In fact, when I returned home from the hospital after giving birth to my son and saw that all of my valuables were missing from my home, I was comforted by Psalm 23, knowing He would always be there to protect me. Even when I got myself into terrible situations due to my willful blindness, God always provided a way for me, and I am eternally grateful.

Today, I am divorced, but my ex-husband and I are still friends. My son is the light of my life. Every year, he is his university's highest academic achiever; I thank God every day that I was blessed to have him in my life. Though my life has been a struggle at times, I am so thankful for the relationship I have built with God and myself. We may have to go through terrible times in our lives, but remember that you *will* make it through! You will be victorious! For me, nothing compares to that feeling of victory, which pushed me to try something completely new: publishing an uplifting online magazine, Victorious Magazine. I could only have done it through the support and strength of God, reminding me that if you want to please God, walk on water. You don't have to know everything or be perfect; He is begging you to come to Him. If you do take that first step, He will reward you for your faith. He keeps His promises, and He will love you forever and ever and ever.

W.O.W. - Words of Wisdom

And provide for those who grieve in Zion— to bestow on them a crown of beauty instead of ashes...

– Isaiah 61:3a, NIV

When you make God the first priority in your life before anyone else, He will show you who you really are and who you are meant to be. Do not let anyone define you, or live in anyone's shadow. Do not let anyone dim your light. God will never leave or forsake you. Seek His face, and talk to Him because He has a great plan for your life if you will only allow Him to transform you. In every way, acknowledge God and see the beauty in the waiting season. The waiting season teaches patience, which works a perfect work in you, and forgiveness, which sets you free to move forward and to forget. Through God's processing, He will make beauty out of the pain you endured, exchanging His beauty for the ashes of heartbreak.

Tracy Shy Simmons began singing age 2 at her grandfather's church In Wilmington Delaware. Age 13, She formed the group, "Tracy and The Melodies," gaining popularity touring the east coast and recording radio Interviews. Tracy joined, and later became lead vocalist for The Hall of Famed Wilmington Chester Mass Choir. Tracy led the hit song "Over there" which is viewed on the "Best of The Stellar Awards." She also sang and wrote for Tremaine Hawkins, touring London, Bahamas, and USA. Tracy has toured extensively to Europe, South America, and Scandinavian countries.

She performed in Tyler Perry's hit stage play "Behind Closed Doors," and T D Jakes' "Woman thou art loosed." Tracy is a Humanitarian Award recipient, Best Female Vocalist Competition, Champion Award of Delaware, and Outstanding Women in Ministry by Black National Congress. Her solo albums include "Tracy Shy Live," "So Much More." You Love Me" is due for release.

My Children, My Legacy

By: Wendy K. Smith

* * *

This story is dedicated to those feeling lost or like they have no purpose in life. I hope that it gives someone the courage to keep their head up and keep going.

As a mother, I often reflect back on my childhood which wasn't all flowers and rainbows. I had parents that divorced when I was ten years old and grew up with my mom, who did what she could to provide for me, but we struggled a lot. There were weeks we couldn't even afford meat. Many things were hard to come by, but it was those tough times in life that made me stronger and want to be different.

My mother was bipolar and she didn't believe she had a problem or tried to get help for it. It can be very hard living with someone with this awful disease. It was difficult for me to make, let alone, *keep* friends because we moved a lot. At one point, we lived in a trailer and had a room that was the size of a walk-in closet. It leaked over my bed every time it rained. When I would have friends over, my mom would forget that she said they could come and would get very upset with me, lock herself in the bathroom and say she was going to hurt herself. This was the norm in my life. Most times, at a young age, I was the adult and she was the child in the relationship. I tried to take care of and felt sorry for her. My brother lived with my dad and had a better, more stable life. He had a bicycle, nice clothes, a dry bed and food on the table. These were little things to most, but also things that most people take for granted.

I eventually ended up living with my grandma for a while, because my mom got a job working 3rd shift. My grandma and I were very close. I used to watch her put her makeup on every morning while she got ready for work. We watched *Dallas* and *Dynasty* soap operas, ate Fiddle Faddle and went to church together every Sunday. I loved getting dressed up for church and then eating at the local restaurant in the mall. I got involved in the bible study group at church and even learned all the books of the Bible. This was such a wonderful bonding time for me and my grandma. It brought us closer together and to God. These memories will always be close to my heart.

A few years later, after moving back with my mom, my dad ended up getting custody of me because my home life wasn't stable. My dad realized that while he was paying child support, I didn't seem to have decent clothes or a proper roof over my head. He knew my life wouldn't end up well if I remained with my mom. It was a huge adjustment moving in with my dad, as he had a new wife and I was living with my brother. There were some changes in this household such as stricter house rules, extra school work and household chores. I also couldn't talk about my mom without my dad or stepmom getting upset. I was really sad and worried about my mom because again, I had been the adult and she was the child in our relationship. My dad decided to take me to counseling. Even though I knew it was better for me in the long run to be living with him, I still felt guilty for leaving my mom.

My self-esteem and confidence were at an all-time low, so my dad thought it would be beneficial for me to attend a modeling school. I went on to graduate from Barbizon Modeling and did really well. I started to get paying jobs and before long, I was focused on swimsuit modeling. I was so proud of myself for overcoming my fears and building my confidence. But my dad kept pushing me to aspire for more.

My dad told me I couldn't rely on my looks to get me through life. It's funny because I wasn't doing that. I was just so happy to not be insecure and lack the self confidence that kept me from doing the things I wanted. I was finally free and confident. The more modeling jobs I got, the more my stepmom became upset and talked negatively about every shoot I landed. I didn't let it bring me down and kept going. Her and my dad had three more kids of their own and it seemed like all of her affections were reserved for her kids. My dad wasn't "allowed" to give me much of his time, especially with my extra activities. It was tough.

I couldn't wait to leave for college. My grades were awesome and I did great in school. My best friend's parents loved me and showed that love to me, but I never felt loved by my dad and stepmom. When I was filling out scholarship applications, I was told by my stepmom that I was wasting my time because I wouldn't get any scholarships. Not only did I get a scholarship, I got three. Again, I was so proud of myself.

I resolved that if I ever had kids, I was never going to be like either of my parents. I sought out counseling, digging deep to the root of my issues so I could get past all the pain and hurt I'd been through. I don't say this for sympathy, but for hope and strength for someone else who may be going through a similar situation. Your past doesn't have to define your path or story.

I continued to live with my dad and stepmother for the latter part of my teenage years. They were more stable and provided clothes on my back and food on the table. They made sure I did well in school. However, every time I was told that I wouldn't be good at something by my family or naysayers, I just pushed and worked harder, being the best I could be at everything I did. This is why I am who I am today. I used every challenge to make me stronger.

Many years later, I have the most beautiful, athletic, smart and precious children and mother-in-law I could ask for. My daughter reminds me of myself at her age. She has had her ups and downs in life and has faced many challenges as a teenager, but still manages to come out stronger in the end. Still, it hasn't been easy for her.

I chose to be the mother and kind of supporter my children needed me to be, so they could do or be what they wanted to be. Both of my kids are great basketball players, but they found the sport to be too cutthroat and competitive as a whole. One day while my daughter and I were at the YMCA exercising on the rowing machines, I mentioned that she would be good at rowing. She looked into rowing and joined a nearby rowing club. My other children grew to love the sport as well.

The rest of this story is history. That fall, my daughter received two gold medals. She trained so hard and fell in love with her rowing team. She said she'd found her family. The rowing club was a 45-minute drive from our home, but I knew how important rowing was to my children. They needed a strong support system to be successful. My kids worked out six days a week and worked hard when they did. They are so dedicated and I am so proud of them. Rowing was their outlet at a time when other sports weren't so nice. Being involved in a sport in which they worked hard and loved made me happy.

My life has taught me that we don't have to let the negative things in life define us. We can change and be better than the way we were taught or raised. Only we can define ourselves and make the decision to be the best parents, spouses, friends, workers or children we can be. My daughter has broken two world records and is the number one rower in the country for her age. She leaves for California this summer to be on the nationals' team, all because she never gave up and had the unconditional support of her parents. My kids are my legacy and they are my *why* every single day. What's your *Why*?

W.O.W. - Words of Wisdom

It's what you do in the dark that puts you in the light.

- Michael Phelps

These words from one of my daughter's favorite athletes encourage us to work hard every day towards our goals and dreams, and we will be rewarded. We must not be boastful or brag, but do the work that's required to be successful.

Wendy Smith is the proud owner of a health and wellness social retail company that provides clean living products that help your body live to its fullest potential. As an advocate for health and fitness most of her life she loves to inspire others and help them on their health journey.

She loves to motivate and inspire other women to become entrepreneurs as she was one herself for 23 years, owning her own Home Staging Business, which included organizing, decluttering, staging, interior design, and cleaning of homes to get them ready to sell.

Wendy also helps with Redemption Rescue, a pet rescue, which rescues homeless and injured pets from shelters and other surrendering organizations.

Leading by Example

By: Dagmar Torres

* * *

I always speak about my military career because the lessons I learned in the armed forces strengthened my character and professional development – both as a civilian employee and an entrepreneur. I can say that the words "We Lead by Example" were permanently engraved into my mind during and beyond my 24 years of military service.

During my years of service, I went through many trials, and each time – just like the Israelites through the Exodus – I called upon God to help me. By the year 2000, I had accepted Yehoshua (Jesus) as my Lord and Savior and got baptized. Yet, I could never imagine His plans for me and the trials He would allow me to live through.

One of the most significant trials happened between the years 2006 and 2009. I moved from Puerto Rico to the state of Virginia due to a civilian job I landed. I moved days before my 30th birthday; count 30 days later, and my mom passed away. It hit hard because I did not get to say goodbye or be there by her side. All I can say is that I am thankful that we were on good terms.

As I started to heal from the loss, I submerged myself in my J.O.B. (Joyless Occupational Bondage) and found myself satisfied with the pay. I was grateful I was making enough to survive, and work kept my mind occupied. During those years, I served simultaneously in the Army Reserves. I had no close friends in Virginia and still was adjusting to the new environment while assigned to my military unit in Puerto Rico. I had to travel every month to the island to comply with my military duties. That period was, without a doubt, the busiest and loneliest time of my life.

Months passed of me traveling back to Puerto Rico, and my father had a stroke, making things even more difficult. I was still transitioning between the two locations. I relied on friends to get around those days. I was offered help from someone who swore to be my friend, and I accepted.

Little did I know that he would betray my trust. Every time I think about it now, I imagine what Yehoshua felt when Judas betrayed him. That feeling of disappointment competed with many others as soon as that "man," that animal raped me.

A rollercoaster of emotions went through me. I felt guilty because I let my guard down. I felt ashamed, dirty. I sought no help. I crumbled inside. Torn by my circumstances, bound by my military orders and hopeless, I bottled up my emotions just to be shattered inside eleven months later when my father died. I cried so much, and, to make things worse, I had nobody to talk to. The two central figures in my life had departed forever.

You must be asking yourself, what does this have to do with leadership? Well, it has to do with everything. Any negative or traumatic experience affects an individual's ability to believe in themselves. Studies like Teunissen and Bok in 2013 prove that people's internal entity beliefs affect their goal-setting skills.[1] Therefore, we cannot lead people if we live full of worthlessness, anger, fear, hate and hopelessness.

Holding on to pain causes more pain. I felt like an impostor when I had to counsel someone or show strength for my peers and subordinates. An emotional storm brewed within me during those years. But I knew I had two choices:

1) Let my situation control me; or

2) Take control of the problem.

I opted for option two. But my solution was to bottle up my emotions, and in the meantime, I did what we all do when catastrophe crosses our path. I cried out to God, blamed God, fought with God, asked God for forgiveness and started the cycle all over again.

I felt guilty for letting my guard down and becoming a statistic.[2] Although, today, I know that what happened to me was not because of how I looked or dressed. Today, I know it was not my fault and that I am not the only one. Unfortunately, every 98 seconds, a child, man or woman is sexually assaulted in the United

---

[1] Teunissen, P. W., & Bok, H. G. (2013). Believing is seeing: how people's beliefs influence goals, emotions and behaviour. Medical education, 47(11), 1064-1072.

[2] Over 80% of sexual assaults are committed by an acquaintance and 69% of rape victims in the US are women aged between 12 to 34 years old. Source: https://legaljobsite.net/sexual-assault-statistics/

States[3], which means that every 98 seconds, a person suffers an attack, not only to their body but to their dignity.

Many will not fully recover from a sexual assault, but some will recover and – like myself – will share their testimony with the hope of helping at least one person heal. To inspire them to turn that pain into fuel. Because if it can't kill you, it can build you. This is when I looked at the crucifixion and the example of leadership Yehoshua set for us.

He endured flogging, mocking and the most brutal execution a human body could bear. Yet, He did not quit – not only so for God's promise to be fulfilled – but so we could be saved. As I looked at His crucifixion, I found three parallels that tell us how we are to handle our troubles.

First, we are to take our sins, tribulations and pains and place them at Yehoshua's feet. Because when we surrender to Him, He dwells within us, setting us free (Galatians 5:1); and, to surrender, we need to let go of what causes pain so He can heal us.

Secondly, at the cross, men took Yehoshua's body but could not touch His soul nor stop Him from fulfilling His purpose. Therefore, my assailant had my body, but could not take away my soul and my purpose.

---

[3] Vagianos, A. (2017, April 06). 30 alarming statistics that show the reality of sexual violence In America. Retrieved from https://www.huffpost.com/entry/sexual-assault-statistics_n_58e24c14e4b0c777f788d24f

Third, death could not stop Yehoshua as He rose from death. Therefore, we are also called to rise from our emotional and spiritual death. We enter a stage of emotional and spiritual death (especially after being raped) when we stop loving life and our Creator.

It took me some years to conclude that I needed to bury my tribulations and have an emotional and spiritual awakening to rise by renewing my relationship with Yahweh – our Creator – and loving life by having a close relationship with Him. To allow this awakening to occur, I had to set myself free from the self-blame, anxiety, low self-esteem, anger, fear and isolation caused by the assault. I had to forgive myself for misplacing my trust and forgive him who trespassed against me. Not an easy task, but it was the only way to rise, move on and lead others.

As a success strategist, I could not hold on to those negative feelings and lead others to success. Moreover, I could not let God's light shine through me if I did not set myself free from darkness. Consequently, leading by example requires that we embody our message and show others how to overcome hard times by walking the walk. Leading by example requires us to let go of what holds us back from rising.

Today, I challenge you to give yourself freedom and unlock your leadership potential by leading by example, as Yehoshua did.

W.O.W. - Words of Wisdom

Every test that comes upon you is normal for human beings. But God is faithful: he won't let you be tested beyond your ability. Along with the testing, he will provide the way of escape, so that you can bear it.

— 1 Corinthians 10:13, NTE

Yehoshua (Jesus) set the example of leadership for humanity to follow. If we live as He did, we can help people succeed and overcome their circumstances. The only way to stop hurting is by placing your pain at the cross. If it can't kill you, it can build you! If you don't let the situation control you, you choose to let the problem positively shape you. Leading by example requires you to release yourself from negative emotions.

Dagmar Torres is a retired Army Veteran with over 24 years of leadership experience and eight years in network marketing. She is known as the Success Strategist. Dagmar's formal education consists of a bachelor's degree in political sciences and a master's in social sciences with a major in criminology. Dagmar's understanding of human behavior provides her with a wealth of knowledge applicable for personal and entrepreneurial development.

During the pandemic of 2020, Dagmar turned into coaching to fulfill the need people had to reinvent themselves in the digital world. Currently, Dagmar helps entrepreneurs create a synchronized brand, create high levels of online engagement, and achieve follower-to-client conversion. She also produces and hosts a weekly podcast, the Be Fearless, where she features success stories of people that went from ordinary to extraordinary.

Dagmar enjoys reading, traveling, and long walks with her four-legged son Reggie.

Manifest a Greater Destiny

By: Toni Moore Esq.

* * *

Make no mistake: I am no one's victim. Despite growing up in church, I was abused throughout my childhood, wherein most of the worst things that could ever happen to a girl happened to me. I didn't like the victim story I was born into, so I repeatedly tried to change it. I didn't like the notion of not having enough because of the decisions my mother made throughout her life. So I kept trying to convince her to change her story so that our stories could be better. By the time I reached my preteen years, I had grown weary of running with Mama to rescue shelters for battered women, resorting to food banks for sustenance and living with outstretched hands in hopes that others would fill them; I refused to play the victim role.

Because of my traumatized beginnings, I thought happily ever after was a person, place or thing that was beyond my reach. Because of my limited knowledge about who I was and the potential for greatness I had within myself, I just thought if I was pretty or smart enough, my Prince Charming would take me far, far away from the people that made my life a living hell. But Prince Charming didn't come fast enough for me, nor did the record contracts, modeling contracts or anything else that could help me get away from the life I knew. So I did what others do without a plan, purpose and goal: I scratched and survived in a life that was beneath my godly privileges. More than one too many times, I found myself desperately asking God to help me escape the financial and romantic entanglements in which I should have never been engaged in the first place. Much like a tide of water on the sandy beach, I was so far removed from the church girl who wanted to be an evangelist (that I used to be), I didn't recognize myself.

In my wiser years, I've learned that many women find themselves trying to fabricate a fairy tale from life experiences and circumstances they fell into, stumbled onto or desperately pursued based on what they perceived to be true. Much like me, they were forced to live a life they didn't choose but were still forced to live nonetheless. Based on their life experiences, some women grew up believing that they were given life to be objectified instead of glorified. In contrast, some women grew up to believe that love is a battlefield in which they must deny their wants to live peacefully. And still another group of women love and praise God, but when it comes to their day-to-day living, they don't trust Him enough to help them live a better life. In effect, most women are not satisfied with the life they're given nor do they know how to manifest the life they believe they deserve and desire. I'm raising my hand to profess my guilt.

As a self-help junkie who grew up in church, I realized that more was possible. Throughout scripture and life, I saw proof that God could allow us to fulfill a greater destiny despite traumatic beginnings. And because God did it for others, I knew He was more than able to help me change my realities. However, I knew within my mind that mere self-help wouldn't work. After all, I was a walking epistle of positive thoughts, meditations and hope with an added bonus of grit to make life happen. But no matter how hard I tried to make the mountain move, it just sat there. So when my life became too much to bear, I did the unthinkable, asking God to show up and show me what He was made of.

Similarly, if the life you live does not reflect your hopes, dreams and prayers, you must shift your position. No matter what you did to sabotage yourself, give yourself permission to go beyond welfare, welts, bruises, failures and disillusionment. Don't allow yourself to stay in the gutters of society or live within the shadows of your possibility. No matter who didn't help, who won't help, who sees you as competition and who only sees you in your messy state, don't stay stuck in your mess. Whether you were a traumatized child, hopeless victim, promiscuous woman, utter failure or worthless sinner, give yourself permission to be a better version of yourself. Be the woman of your dreams by positioning yourself to be the person who is more than enough to be, do and have more. Just know, when you are given an opportunity to live, love and achieve more than you've ever seen or heard before, take it. Don't just try it out! Commit to the dream and advocate for your future possibilities. Never forget, you are fearfully and wonderfully made to create— including a life that you believe you deserve and desire. Allow the words of your mouth and the meditations of your heart to manifest better, greater and more for yourself.

Don't waste time or get stuck with people who refuse to rise higher. Similarly, don't limit yourself to people who only tolerate you so that they can use your gifts, talents and abilities. As long as you are not expecting anything, you will not elevate yourself. Instead, you will subconsciously accept what shows up in life. You must be your own advocate. You must set your own boundaries to ensure you don't offer your pearls to swine. Even if you find yourself serving as your one and only cheerleader, seek better for *you*. You must embrace and nurture your best attributes to emerge as the fullest version of yourself. No matter how much your heart aches for acceptance, bet on yourself. Don't diminish your shine or play small because others don't fully appreciate the gift of your life. Instead, double down on your blessings until you defy reality.

God gave you a mandate to change the world around you; it is time for you to seek and know what more can be. While there are no clear-cut rules regarding the process of becoming who God says you are, success leaves clues. Within each moment of every day, empower yourself to be the queen of your destiny. Give yourself permission to enlarge your territory. Give yourself permission to win by any means necessary. Give yourself permission to defy the status quo. Go to school, say yes to the job, create the business, buy and sell stock, own real estate property. Give yourself permission to go up the social ladder, climb the corporate ladder and then make your *own* ladders. Take a leap to change the trajectory of your destiny. Don't be the saboteur of your success because no one lets you be the woman of your dreams.

Untether, unleash and up level yourself so that you can position yourself in alignment with people, places and things that can help you manifest greater things.

W.O.W. - Words of Wisdom

As a man thinketh, so is he.

— Proverbs 23:7a, KJV

Elevate your mindset and with God, you can be and do all things. Focus your thoughts on becoming the higher version of yourself, and with Him, you can manifest a greater legacy and destiny.

Toni Moore is an Intellectual Property and Business Attorney. She is one of the leading attorneys and business strategists who coach, advice and challenge women to live more powerfully in every aspect of their lives.

Throughout a professional career spanning more than 20 years, Toni has worked at financial firms, mid-level law firms, large firms, colleges, universities, federal agencies, churches and faith-based organizations. She currently operates the Moore Legal Firm and Sheleader Consulting to empower women to build wealth through entrepreneurship.

Her Signature Talks include Boss Up, Legalize Your Side Hustle, Handle Your Business, Protect Your Assets.

@tonimooreesq; Contact: info@legallychic360.com

Bring Out Your Inner Leader

By: Janet Walters

Growing up, I believed everything my family told me. My dad said I was dumb, stupid, dizzy and addlepated, and that was when he was home. I didn't see him very often. He spent a lot of time drinking and shooting the breeze with the guys after work. However, those names stuck with me for many years.

My mother said I was average. I didn't speak until I was four. She took me to doctor after doctor. She thought I was autistic, mentally ill or had hearing problems. I was painfully shy and used to hide in corners, hoping my brothers would just leave me alone. My three brothers didn't like me because I was a girl. I was "less than" in their eyes. I tried to fit in with them, but I wasn't welcomed. It turned out that I didn't have any illness or disabilities, yet I bought into the belief that I was below average.

During my years in school, I was a C or D student. Whenever I brought home my report cards, I'd set them on the kitchen table to wait for someone to look at them. I noticed my parents never reviewed them or talked to me about my low grades. My mother just signed my report cards and told me to give them to the teacher.

When I was 13, I wanted to make some extra money. My mother was a miniature schnauzer dog handler. She also bred and groomed them. We had an old schnauzer named Cindy. When Cindy was 13 or 14 years old, I asked my mother if I could help her wash her dogs to make some extra money. She said yes and gave me Cindy to bathe. When I sprayed her with warm water, she snapped at me. Water sprayed on the walls and floor. My mother got mad and told me I did a terrible job. She threw two quarters at me and said I would never wash her dogs again. I hated my mom, dad and three brothers. My wish was to get away from my family as soon as possible.

At the age of 15, I wanted to live with my friend Jeannine and her mom. Everyone called her *mom* because she was cool. Although it was the 70's, Mom dressed like she was in the 60's, wearing pedal pushers and sleeveless tops with poufy auburn hair in a high ponytail. We partied on beer and cigarettes with the girls and guys at Mom and Jeannine's house, at the beach and in the mountains.

One day, I told Mom about my family, and she said I could live with her and Jeannine. I told my mom that I was going to live with them. "Absolutely not," my mother said. Eventually she made my wish come true. She kicked me out of the house when I was 17. She said I was having too much fun at the beach (my friends and I were always going to Santa Monica or Zuma Beach often). "Get out of my house and get a job." I had no choice but to leave. She changed the locks so I couldn't get in.

I left the nonsense behind, but I took the anxiety and resentment with me. I was so anxious that I never spoke up or spoke out. I was too scared to make a mistake or be put down. I gave the people in my life, my all. I was tired of trying to win their approval. It was never enough.

Later, I decided to earn my bachelor's degree. *I'll show my family!* I thought. It turned out no one cared. Not one person in my family came to my graduation. I soon learned my degree didn't solve my limiting beliefs.

These beliefs continued to impact me in my professional years. I saw many growth opportunities at my job. But I avoided talking to people. I never spoke up, even though I wanted to contribute to the discussions. I dummied down because I didn't want to stand out and speak about anything because I feared being criticized by others.

I was tired of laying low in the background. I felt ill-equipped. Yet I heard the voice in my head tell me, *you're made for so much more. Do something different. Do something new.* I decided to get my master's degree in Management.

Six months later, during my new class, my professor told us we'd be giving a 15-minute presentation in three weeks about our future selves in five years. My mind shouted, *what?! Speak in front of my professor and everyone else?* I was ready to bolt out of the classroom--but I stayed. After class, I told my professor about my fear of public speaking and offered to do another project instead of giving the presentation. She said, "Janet, the only way you will ever get over the fear of public speaking is to speak in public." She gave me an extra credit assignment: visit a Toastmasters club and attend the meeting. I'd give a one-to-three-minute speech in front of the class and tell everyone about what I learned at my Toastmasters meeting.

Meanwhile, I was working full-time while attending grad school. I also continued working on my communication/public speaking skills at my Toastmasters club. While I didn't realize it at first, I was also developing my leadership skills. I began participating in meetings at work. I became more assertive with my colleagues. I spoke more truthfully with others.

At work, everyone feared this particular executive--except for a few of his colleagues. He asked me why my boss didn't send her report to him, which was due three days ago. In the past, I would've crumbled and stammered, "I don't know. Uhhhh she's busy." Instead, I said, "She's in Indonesia. You approved her business trip, correct?" He said, "Oh yeah. I did, didn't I?" I asked him if he'd like me to email my boss to remind her to send her status report. He said, "Never mind. I need to talk to her anyway." He turned on his heels and closed the door behind him. My colleague Shirley saw the whole conversation. She asked, "Janet, how did you talk to the Big Boss like that?!"

Through that experience, I learned that being a leader isn't about being overbearing, bossy and making people feel scared. Leaders act decisively to resolve challenges without blaming their team members. If a team member fails, the leader fails. I build my self-confidence by becoming more visible and willing to help others without expecting anything back. I volunteered to take the lead on doing the tasks others avoided. Were these tasks glamorous?

No. Did doing these tasks make me look like I was someone important? No. Leadership is not all about looking good. It's about taking the initiative. I disagreed when needed. I wasn't a "Yes" woman. I took charge as a leader by speaking up and taking the initiative.

I didn't need a title to be a leader. At my job, I became a leader by going above and beyond my job description. I made phone calls to the community and others. I attended off hours' events. When I saw my colleagues in deadline mode, I helped them by making copies, preparing invoices and packages to be mailed or by courier service. I gave presentations. I admit, it was intimidating to speak in front of people, especially when they glared at me with their arms folded or were focused on their phones (Blackberries were all the rage at the time).

While I was learning and growing at my job, I was learning, growing and serving in leadership with the Toastmasters organization. A few years later, I was presented with a growth opportunity. The top leader of our organization asked if I'd be interested in serving in directorship. Absolutely! I quickly learned I'd be continually embarking on unknown territory and stepping out of my comfort zone for a minimum of three years.

You can't jump over, avoid or run away from fear. You can't walk sideways around it or even crawl underneath it. The only way to overcome fear is to go through it. As a businesswoman and entrepreneur, I've learned, continue to study and work on how to become a better speaker, stepping out of my comfort zone with improved critical thinking and time management skills.

You are a leader! Your parents, teachers, siblings, well-meaning friends and colleagues might have said unkind words, made fun of you or told you lies about yourself. Just because they said or did those things, doesn't mean that they represent your true self. Remember, God is in charge. Don't let anyone stop you from living the life that God has put in your heart. He's always there for you. As a believer, you're more than a conqueror.

W.O.W. - Words of Wisdom

Do not worry about anything, but in everything by prayer and supplication with thanksgiving let your requests be made known to God. And the peace of God, which surpasses all understanding, will guard your hearts and your minds in Christ Jesus.

- Philippians 4:6, ESV

When you focus on God, anything is possible. You can be a leader, regardless of your past. All you have to do is lay your fears and insecurities at the feet of the Father, and He will give you the peace you need to excel.

Janet Walters is an Empowerment and Motivation Strategist. She helps women realize their greatness, get clear on their goals and know they have the power to empower and motivate themselves and others. Additionally, she is the business owner of a health and wellness company where she shares the benefits of health and wellness consciousness. Through Toastmasters, she learned to overcome her fear of public speaking, and started her leadership journey in 2007.

She is also a Past District Director in Toastmasters. She led her district of 3,000 people in achieving number one ranking in the US and Western hemisphere and number 10 globally. Janet firmly believes that having a vision, making a plan, taking action and never giving up are the keys to success in all areas of life.

Janet also gives speeches and conducts workshops on the topics of leadership, motivation, volunteerism, re-invention, and life fulfillment.

A Legacy worth Fighting For

By: Pastor Uchenna Lewis

* * *

There comes a time in everyone's life when the question is asked: what is this journey called life all about? When it's all said and done, how will we be remembered? What type of mark will we leave on the earth? If you have ever asked any of these questions, I welcome you to a journey, one of unearthing and strategically building a legacy worth fighting and leaving for the next generation.

March 24, 2010, it was a hair before 6am. I am sure you probably do not remember the happenings of that day, but for me, it will remain a day forever etched in my memory. *Knock knock.* Hmmm... That may have been a figment of my imagination or a symptom of no sleep which of course comes with being a nursing mother of an almost three-month-old. *Knock knock* again! This time, I turned to my then husband and asked, "Are you expecting any delivery or anyone this morning? This early?"

"Of course not," he replied. But there was the knock again, and this time he jumped out of bed and scurried downstairs to find out who would dare rudely persist to get an audience with us so early without as much as a prior call. The baritone nature of the voice that spoke next indicated that our door knocker was a man. 'Are you Christian Okobi?' he asked; to which Chris responded in the affirmative. The line of questioning continued but this time, the voice seemed nearer, like the man had now entered our home. I jumped off the bed, put on my robe, grabbed my baby and hurried down the stairs to see what in the world this was all about. I made my way down the stairs to find my home had been invaded by ICE. In utmost dismay, I look at my then husband and father of my child in disbelief. "What's going on?!" I screamed exasperatedly. It was honestly more of a plea than a question, to which lifting his head, he looked me square in the eyes and responded with words that up until that point were my worst nightmare. "They came for me," he said, head down. I felt the floor beneath me literally give way, the wind totally knocked out of my lungs for what felt like an eternity. I was brought back to reality by the words of the only female ICE officer who approached me and said, "Ma'am, please calm down... I need you to have a seat, especially with the baby in your arm." The rest of the encounter was barely a blur.

Time will not permit me to explain all of the details of what led to that life changing day. But I can say this was not the life we anticipated just the day before, as we celebrated the birthday of the one who was now being snatched away. Oh, and did I mention our baby? The miracle I held in my arms. The miracle we had believed God for, for almost five years. Close to five years of waiting, God answered... and now this? I went from boom to bust in less than 24 hours. My entire world was plainly crumbling before me!

What do you do when things fall apart, and the center which held you together no longer seems to hold true? How do you recover from having to run outside at 2:30 am with your baby in your arms, after the repo man, because life suddenly had become a living nightmare? What would you do if you went from having it all to being stripped down to faith, belief and a hunger for a better day? What do you do when you realize that perhaps, the hell that had been unleashed, seemingly causing you to lose it all, just might be an indication that it is time to fight... fight like hell for YOUR LEGACY!

Your story may not exactly be like mine, but you are probably either in a fight or about to encounter one. You are not holding this book in your hands by coincidence. In my fight season, I made up my mind that devastation was not my destiny. Being in a space where I had nothing left but my faith and the gift of a newborn child made me awaken to my purpose. I awakened to the fact that I was created for more, and therefore had the divine responsibility to leave an imprint, not only on the new life that I held in my hands, but on the many others that I had yet to meet. I awakened to the call of LEGACY!

The lowest points of your life are designed to *make you* choose to build a stronger legacy. I am on assignment to stir you to make a choice: accept the devastation and wallow in defeat, or rise up to FIGHT FOR YOUR LEGACY! It is your choice!

Legacy begins with the end in mind. We have the onus to think of the lives we are living and building and what that entails for those we love when we are no longer here. I was confronted with the fact that if anything were to happen to me, the child God gave me would have little or nothing to live a better life than I had been afforded. The idea of building a legacy must be founded on running our leg of the race and making sure we give a leg up to the ones to whom we are handing the baton. They must be equipped to run faster and further because of all we endured before them. Up until that fateful turning point, I had allowed myself to be in a position where I had built nothing and had nothing financially. And the truth is, most of us need to face that stark reality; sometimes it takes a make-or-break situation to deal with these hard truths.

Today, as a pastor and minister of the Gospel of Jesus Christ, I know all too well what it means to shepherd people, minister to them and sadly, sometimes witness them in their last moments of life face the sad reality that they've left the family they loved and cared about with an empty bag. As a matter of fact, sometimes the bag is so empty that the family ends up having to pull funds together from friends, family and strangers to afford the opportunity to put the remains of their loved ones away somewhat gracefully. A legacy of debt is left behind for the people who are supposed to be surviving *loved* ones.

This is a story we know all too well, especially within the African American and African community. And truth be told, this too may very well have been my story if I was not accosted with the reality of the fact that I was headed down the same road unless I did something and did it fast. Even though I was daily serving God and

His people, I knew there had to be more. I had to first exemplify the reality that more was possible. I had to also make sure that I knew and had a plan for the type of legacy I wanted to build and leave behind. Yes, I was already building a spiritual legacy of faith and leading people to live for God and plan for eternity with Him. But why would we normalize the idea of being *sold out to go to Heaven* while leaving hell on earth for the people we love? The idea of seeing people repeat cyclical pathologies that lend themselves to create generations of individuals totally ill-advised and oblivious to the fact that financial freedom and generational wealth is possible, left me pained and seeking God for a way to sound the alarm amongst His children, and most importantly within our community. This reality led me to my quest and journey headlong into financial literacy. I needed to know more so I could do more. I needed to learn a different way of doing so I could experience a different way of being. This was achievable through intention, education and implementing purposeful strategy.

I want to share with you five keys that are needed for the fight to build a legacy of faith and financial freedom:

1. Make sure your life and death will not be in vain. Your living should be impactful and so should your transition to glory. For this to be a reality, someone must pay the price for a legacy of financial freedom. If no one within your family has paid that price, make up your mind to do so and pass on the

mindset to the next generation. Legacy requires sacrifice and intention, therefore you must first determine that no matter where you are today, you will not leave this earth without a strong legacy. The following steps will help you get a better footing.

2. Understand that provision that does not outlive your earthly presence is irresponsible. Proverbs 13:22 (NKJV) tells us: "A good man leaves an inheritance to his children's children." This verse keeps our life goals, vision and legacy front and center when we are choosing how to use our finances and resources today. If you were to breathe your last breath, what type of legacy will be left for your children and grandchildren? Is there an inheritance in place for them? If the answer is no, you can start today.

3. Reverse engineer generational wealth by investing in a life insurance policy. I surmise that this is the foundational strategy for leaving a legacy of financial freedom. No other portfolio or strategy yields the dividends nor offers the benefits that the right policy will. You must attach more value to your life than you do your things. How much do you pay monthly for your auto insurance? Is it more than you put aside for your life insurance? The answer to this question might help you see where you place more value. Reach out or speak to a trusted licensed financial professional who will guide and help you figure out the right plan for you and your family.

4. Do not fall victim to consumerism. No, you do not need every new purse nor do you need to keep up with the Joneses. Save more than you spend; you never know the day when all hell will break loose. Make sure you have an emergency fund. Your savings account should far outweigh your checking account. Proverbs 21:20 (NKJV) tells us: "The wise store up choice food and olive oil, but fools gulp theirs down."

5. Give more than you receive. This is a tried-and-true principle. The more you give, the more you will have to give. Proverbs 11:24-25 (NKJV) states: "One gives freely yet grows richer; another withholds what he should give, and only suffers want. Whoever brings blessing will be enriched, and one who waters will himself be watered."

Today, I am thankful to walk alongside many and offer them guidance that is needed to leave a legacy of faith and financial freedom, offering comfort and wisdom because of the things I have suffered. Everything you have been through was not just for you. The following generation that will run the next leg of the race needs you to run this leg with tenacity. Make wise decisions and fight like crazy to help them run their legs better, faster and further than you. Your legacy is worth the fight!

W.O.W. - Words of Wisdom

Therefore we also, since we are surrounded by so great a cloud of witnesses, let us lay aside every weight, and the sin which so easily ensnares us, and let us run with endurance the race that is set before us, looking unto Jesus, the author and finisher of our faith, who for the joy that was set before Him endured the cross, despising the shame, and has sat down at the right hand of the throne of God.

– Hebrews 12:1, NKJV

As you provide a legacy of financial freedom, you must run your race on earth with endurance, with an end goal in mind. Look to Jesus for strength because He will give you strength to finish strong!

Pastor Uchenna Lewis is a pacesetter known for not catering to the Status Quo. She is a Mother, Wife, Pastor, Prophetic Intercessor, Author, International Speaker, Entrepreneur, Coach and Legacy Strategist. She is the Visionary and Founder of **"L.I.F.E Ambassadors"**, an outreach ministry purposed to raise dynamic intercessors and leaders who change lives with the Love of God that Inspires, and Faith in his word that Empowers. An anointed preacher and dynamic leader, she currently serves as the Executive Pastor of **Restoration Bible Church** headquartered in District Heights, MD under the leadership of her husband and overseer, Bishop Alfie S. Lewis. She is also the President of **RWW (Restored Women of Worth)**, the Women's Ministry arm of Restoration Bible Church.

With over 15 years of entrepreneurship, business, and extensive management background, she has excelled in varied leadership roles. As a Financial Literacy and Legacy Strategist, many within her community have benefitted from her passion for educating and empowering them to set up a Legacy plan for generations to come. She's on a mission to help individuals and families build and leave a legacy of faith and financial freedom. Her divine assignment is to provoke those she encounters to live their lives in obedience to purpose and empower our community to normalize leaving an inheritance for our children's children.

A PHOENIX'S VISION

By: Michelle Snow

It has been said that in order for our true authentic selves, our successful selves, our inner heroes to be exposed to the world and even ourselves, there must be an experience, a gut-wrenching test of sorts. An outer battle with our assigned demons. The overcoming and slaying of the dragon of our trial causes us to simultaneously battle the inner enemy within, whether that be fear, pride or another vice. We have two choices. Fight or flight. We are challenged to rise to the occasion of the enemy without and within. Before my trial arrived, I thought I pretty much slayed all day. In order to be a brown girl thriving and climbing the corporate ladder while lacking the proper support that some of my peers received just by nature of their skin color, I was already a hero in my eyes. But in November 2010, I was faced with a dragon that took me to my knees. Literally. It was that time in my life that I was diagnosed with an illness called sarcoidosis. You may not have heard of this illness or even know how to pronounce it at first glance. I certainly didn't know what it was; not even my doctor knew how to treat it because he hadn't heard of it before. He kindly directed me to another practitioner and colleague. I soon learned that it was life-threatening with no cure. It caused me severe breathing problems, chronic pain and weak taste buds. This affliction could not have come at a worse time.

Prior to being diagnosed, I was laid off from my dream job. The job I had waited my entire career to land. And I was good at it, great at it. But it didn't make me happy. I excelled, surpassing department goals on a weekly basis. If anything, I knew for sure that I was on the path to promotion. Which is why I felt completely blindsided when my position was given to a Caucasian male who was paid more for the same work I was doing. The disappointment crushed me, and I began using casual relationships to ease the pain. Promiscuity was my way of using my body to cushion the pain I was feeling inside. But the more I ran from myself, the more I turned away from God.

To add salt to the wound, I learned about a dark family secret that year. After it was revealed to me, I thought the best way to begin to repair the situation was to expose it. For far too long, the motto *What happens in our house stays in our house* is a mask that encourages familial victims to suffer in silence. My family, who I thought would be relieved and appreciative of my bravery to confront the un-confrontable, resulted into them turning their backs on me, causing further divide between family members. Fortunately, my mother and grandmother were still willing to take me in when my chronic pain made me so weak that I couldn't even walk, bathe or even use the bathroom unassisted. For six months, my grandmother and mother, the women I should have been taking care of, were taking care of me like a little baby. The reality humbled me, leaving me feeling helpless. Just months ago, I was the driven dynamic trailblazer with promise, climbing the corporate ladder of my dreams. Within months, I had lost my health, my job, the broken relationships, most of my family and everything seemed to be slipping through my fingers. As I laid in the bed, day after day, staring at the ceiling fan, sick of the nothingness of the television, I ruminated on the cards I'd been dealt, and I felt downright bitter.

I gripped my anger tightly, not wanting to forgive those who had hurt me. And I probably would have been like that forever. That is, until one day I begin to ask myself this pertinent question: What I was doing with the time I had left? My illness could take my life any day. Was I going to remain resentful until the day I died or was I going to finally give it up to God and ask for healing? I chose the latter because deep down, I didn't want the pain to haunt me anymore. Keeping my heart submerged in hate just wasn't worth it, especially not toward my family. With a mind made up, I began taking the necessary steps to overcome and transform into the giver of light that I envision myself to be. It was a blurry vision, but I was determined to make each step closer until my vision became a clear reality.

My first step was deciding that I wanted to live and triumph over the pain. I decided that my pain would not define me. That was the only way to make the most of my God-given life. Each day was a blessing, and I had to live it to the fullest. My second step was repenting. As I asked God to grant me forgiveness for my sins, I let Him teach me how to forgive others. It was not an instantaneous process, but the more I put my trust in Him, the more He gave me the strength to forgive and remain in that forgiveness.

Next, I had to reimagine myself. After I had forgiven everyone, I miraculously got my strength back so I could support myself while living with my illness. I thanked God for my blessing. I felt like a brand-new woman. But still I needed a new path, a new vision. Although there were aspects of my previous position that I loved, and many that I didn't, I was done pursuing a life that was not tailor-made for my gifts, skillset and further opportunities for growth. Ultimately, I combined my experiences with human resources, church and community service to build a business where I help uplift people who are going through hardships.

The final touch to my reimagining was changing my name to Michelle Snow. My birth name is Nakia and though it's a beautiful name that will always be special to me, it represents my past, the dark part of me that I was once a victim to. Michelle Snow represents a new, powerful version of myself. Now, when "Nakia" does resurrect to pull me back into bad habits, my illness ironically saves me. If I was tempted to go out, drink and get reckless, my fatigue brought on by my illness would take me straight to bed. Though this was a gift I didn't ask for, it was given to me for a reason, so I make sure to use it to keep my life in check. Through all my unwanted struggles, I have been blessed with a fulfilling purpose in serving others who need guidance and most importantly, I like the mythical phoenix was able to see my best self through the fire of my trials and be reborn into my truest self.

W.O.W. - Words of Wisdom

You may ask me for anything in my name, and I will do it.

- John 14:14, NIV

And when you stand praying, if you hold anything against anyone, forgive them, so that your father in heaven may forgive your sins.

- Mark 11:25, NIV

Both verses reflect different parts of my mindset as I went through my journey. When I was able to get back in line with God after putting an end to my bad behaviors, I had no problem asking Him for what I needed. But I struggled the most with forgiveness since I believed that being bitter was the only thing I could do. When I asked God for help, He let me know that in order for me to heal, I had to choose to liberate myself from resentment. If I expected to be forgiven for my sins, it was only fair to grant those around me with the same courtesy.

Don't let resentment for the past block the blessing of your future. Forgive and let go. Forgiveness will allow you the freedom to receive healing.

Michelle Snow is known as the Platinum Connect & Vision to Performance Coach. She is a Philanthropist, Award-Winning Coach, President & Executive Consultant to multiple companies, and Founder of the non-profit "Grow Together Snow Foundation." She also serves as an expert in Visionary Leadership & Professional Growth for educational institutions, corporations, and businesses.

Michelle is recognized by FORBES, Philadelphia City Council, Philadelphia Department of Commerce, and multiple major media. Michelle's corporate and community experience provides her with leverage to serve clients and community as a benchmark in people-growth, strategy and development. Her passion is best expressed through her personal mantra, "Living Epistles Grow Together." In the year 2021, Michelle Snow Company, LLC OFFICIALLY became a Certified Minority-Owned by EMSDC PA-NJ-DE.

michelle@growwithsnow.com
Facebook: Michelle Snow Company, LLC
www.growwithsnow.com

Become the Light

By: Jennifer Elaine Nameth

* * *

Well, hello, beautiful. Can you believe it? We are here on this amazing adventure together, and I am so blessed to share my journey. I must pause and tell you that I was not an overnight success. I must take you back to where I started.

As a young lady at about the age of 11, I was introduced to entrepreneurship. I know you are thinking, *she must be a multi-millionaire now*. Bear with me because my story is a roller coaster. My mom was my encouragement in my childhood years. We shared the ideals of independence and achievement. During this time, I felt it necessary to learn everything I could from anyone who wanted to add value to my life. By 14, I had a plan of how to build an organization and establish an income stream that would pay me in my sleep. Like any young woman, I drew out my dream, my "perfect bedroom".

Hold on, who was I kidding? What does it mean to make money in my sleep? I had yet to have a job or responsibilities beyond a few pets and a bit of chores. I was a sponge for knowledge, if it was a video, live event or a CD, but opening a book was the dreaded to-do. The books on my shelf were glaring at me, and, as dust began to collect on them, I ended up reading one. *How to Win Friends and Influence People* was an amazing book that I read repeatedly during

150

my high school years. However, nothing truly brought me out of my shy and quiet self. I was always the one watching and learning from others. I suppose you could have labeled me the girl who held the wall up. In every room or place, I tried my best to hopefully be unnoticed. Yet, I knew that deep down, speaking events were my favorite. I loved hearing stories of what various people overcame, how they set goals and what caused them to fail and finally, achieve the breakthrough. I was planning my speech that I would give the world when I succeeded and finally got over my shyness. I was going to bless thousands.

At 16, I felt like I had all the knowledge I needed to achieve my dreams. I knew exactly what to say, how to say it, what to say for objection and the best way to invite and close. I knew how to dress, what pens worked best for notes and what book list would give me the edge. By 18, my plan was foolproof, or so I thought. I bet we all have the plan. It looks a bit like the perfect list, the perfect "Hello how are you? Did you know...", the follow-up plan and finally a yes or no before closing. It was exciting how I was never going to be stuck. I had received training from so many millionaires, so there was no way I couldn't run this like the boss I was. I was made for this. I dreamt about it.

Then it tripped me up. The part of the wisdom I had missed this whole time. The golden nugget that I thought was a fool's gold rock. It began to derail me every time I would get on track. You would think I learned from the first failure. In fact, it destroyed my plan for the next thirteen years. I could not overcome this dirty little word, "expectations." I expected that everyone I spoke to would see my passion, fall in love with my fire and be attracted to my light. I thought everyone would swarm me like moths to a porch light. The harsh reality didn't stop me. I hit the first goal. In fact, I accomplished the first 90-day goal. But what I lost was passion. I had become a person who kept lowering their expectations.

Many bad personal choices in my early 20s resulted into what could now be a lessons-learned book just waiting to be written. By my late 20s, I knew that I loved the industry so much, but I couldn't find the passion I had once had until I met my amazing friend, Di. She was the light I craved, the mentor that spoke to me as if everything I was hearing was the first time. I learned that people would never swarm to me unless I first loved them with all of me. Not a crazy co-dependent kind of love, but the kind of love where they know you truly care. Everyone can be friends, but it takes an entirely different mindset to love without expectation. I expected to be the light for many, but I did not know the key to being the light required me to chase and crave the light from a mentor first. The mentor I set out to be required me to surrender my plan and follow my mentor as if I was learning how to crawl. Like that, I released all expectations and married the process. Not the light that brings swarms of people, but the light that loves and shall be the lighthouse for the lost.

My breakthrough was simple; I consistently "married the process and divorced the results." I had no idea this was how I intended to find my passion. Di said, "Many buses will go by, but you need to get on one; this is the bus you have waited for all your life, let's go." I got on the bus in fear, another risk yet with a great friend who loved me first. We unpacked all my false beliefs until I was humble. This allowed me to eliminate expectations and to simply create goals. The end of every month required an evaluation. What worked? What didn't? What should the change be?

I am forever thankful for Di, and now I get to be the mentor I dreamed of. How can that be? Well, I live in her light, and now my light is brighter because I'm not trying to do it all on my own. Never stop learning, and never become so hard that you think you know it all. Be blessed, and always forgive yourself. This is your journey.

W.O.W. – Words of Wisdom

In my time of walking through the wilderness, I struggled with more than I could have imagined from 2014 to 2019. Feeling defeated, I was reminded of a quote by Thomas Edison: "Our greatest weakness lies in giving up. The most certain way to succeed is always to try just one more time."

At the time, trying one more time seemed impossible. It started with a miscarriage, followed by a job loss, a preeclampsia pregnancy, postpartum depression, third pregnancy, divorce, learning my mom had terminal cancer and that my newborn had chronic kidney disease, and a custody struggle. It was enough to be devastating, but God gave me what was necessary to overcome.

But Jesus beheld them, and said unto them, with men this is impossible; but with God all things are possible.

-    Matthew 19:26, KJV

I was able to stay with my mom full time, have help with my oldest while I took my newborn to hundreds of appointments, became a CNA parent and found my tribe of inspiration from online business. I walked into the best chapter of my life because I tried one more time.

Jennifer E. Nameth, a single mom since 2016, resides in Colorado with her amazing boys, Brayden, 5, and Remington, 4. Having chosen to release her expectations for herself, she now finds herself in the perfect season to walk into the best chapter of her life. With the unwavering faith and armor of God, she managed to defeat what was meant to destroy her.

Blessed with amazing mentorship, she became the leader she was destined to be. She encourages many single moms and dads, helping them with faith-based parenting and business strategies.

Email: jem2015mom@gmail.com

Lost in Paris

By: Stone Love Faure

* * *

Everybody told me not to stay in Paris.

I was locked in my mind, traveling only in my dreams. I needed to go more places than my kitchen and bathroom. I isolated myself due to depression brought on by the passing of my mom. My creative juices were bottled up inside of me. I was ready to pop. I knew I still had youth and wisdom in my body. But I didn't have the courage; time was running out.

I needed to create my legacy and flow. My most functional and contributing years seemed to be passing me by. My first step was to take a step. To make a decision towards something positive and that inspired me. Traveling was my dream. But where would I go, with whom would I go and what did I have to offer? So many questions went through my mind. The questions seemed paralyzing.

The prospect of being away from home for more than two days scared me. My comfort was in my bedroom and my kitchen. I was sleeping too much, and not moving around enough.

Overweight, I was eating through my confusion and emotions. I needed to take a step.

I surfed social media for a few years. I watched the movement of other women creating and living in their flow. I wanted that too. I knew I wasn't there yet. Furthermore, I didn't think I had enough to offer. I began to follow certain influencers who seem to be living their best lives. I reach out to a select few. I was able to develop some relationships with mentors and coaches to help me with my unrealistic fears and unlock some of my potential.

I found my tribe.

I began to journal and eventually got a writing coach. I attended some live women's groups and found other women wanting the same things I did. We began to write together. A woman I respected asked me if I would like to travel to France and take a wisdom course with her. I researched the class and was intrigued. I didn't know how I would do it. But I knew I needed to do it.

I did it. Here's what happened.

I planned to go to dinner, journal and people-watch. I witnessed Parisian culture. I had read about how private the French people were. It felt rather voyeuristic, watching them live their private lives in public. They didn't care that I was in their country alone.

It was Bastille Day weekend, commemorating the storming of the Bastille prison. I rode on the top deck of the Paris Big Tour Bus. The buildings were gothic, gargoyles looming from the rooftops. It was dramatic and picturesque. But I didn't take a single photo. I didn't know the district or the time of day. The uncertainty seemed OK.

I was in Paris.

I hopped off the bus as it pulled away. I saw a brasserie, an outdoor restaurant. I took off my shades and gestured for a table. Intimidated because I wasn't fluent in the language, I didn't speak. I felt invisible.

My trip began with a course in wisdom in Chartres, France. When the classes ended, I decided to rent an apartment in Paris. I took the chance because I knew my experiences and international courses would enhance my coaching practice. I could lead women all over the world through *Stoneology's Retreats*.

I finished eating, relaxing and meditating on the French. But I felt like I was forgetting something. It was my habit of leaving a tip. I remembered the French don't tip after a meal. As an American, it felt like stealing. On occasion, if you're feeling generous, you can leave a euro or two if the service was exceptional.

I walked to the bus stop as night began to fall.

I waited. Attentive and anxious, still the bus never came. With my challenged French, I asked for direction to the Metro to get back to my hotel. Four different times, I got four different recommendations. I was searching and floating amongst what seemed like a bazillion people. But I continued to flow with them. Soon the darkness swallowed up the crowds. The sound of my heels was echoing. I looked behind me to see if something was a threat to me. I couldn't ignore that the tourists were gone. As night completely blanketed the starless sky, the dormant and homeless seemed to appear. My footsteps hurried. They seem to be in sync with my blinks. I couldn't calm down.

My classmate's voices were blaring in my head like carnival music. *Stone, you can't stay in Paris alone.* I began to talk to God. *Father, I'm lost. I know YOU'RE with me. But which way do I go?* I could always feel my mom's presence. I used to live in her belly, and now she lives in my heart. I prayed to them both. My own questions didn't pause for answers.

How was I going to find my way home?

The familiar train stations that were on every corner had vanished. I was a bit relieved when I saw a black man walking towards me. Still, I didn't speak the language. He seemed to get bigger the closer he got. I had to formulate a French phrase. I was unsure. *Please let him speak English.* As he approached I said, "Bon soir, pardon moi monsieure, parlez vous Englais?"

"Bon soir. Yes madam, I speak English."

I took a breath. *Thank you God!* "Could you tell me where the Metro is?"

"Oh no madam, it is too late for you to take the Metro. You must take a taxi." He pointed far to the right. "Do you see this yellow up the way? These are the taxis." I nodded. "Yes, I see. Merci, Monsieur."

"Will you be ok?" he asked. I wanted to cry and say, *I'm not OK*. I smiled and said, "Oh yes, I will be OK." I continued to walk. I was three or four long blocks away.

I appeared to be on an industrial street now. It was motionless. The concrete buildings were covered with French graffiti. Nothing looked familiar. I tried to control my thoughts. But they continued to rally back and forth between my strength and my dread. I felt like running. That seemed reckless. I had to keep my cool and not open the floodgates of fear. So I continued my hurried steps.

The urge to run grew more intense as I got closer to the taxi station. People began to appear again. I wanted to tell somebody I was lost. But my high school French started to merge with my college Spanish. My translations were more like Spanglish babble. What would I say to the taxi driver?

Father, speak for me.

I walked up to the closest cab. I opened my mouth and said through the window, "Eh, Effie Tower." He looked at me and rolled his eyes. (I was in the middle of the taxi lineup.) He continued to read his paper. I took a deep sigh. My heart was beating in my ears. Tears welled up. I slumped to the next taxi. I opened my mouth to say, *Pardon moi, messieur*, but I heard: "Stone!"

I flinched and ducked while looking up and said, "Jesus?"

On another continent, at the moment I needed anybody, not knowing nobody, I heard somebody yell my name. "STONE!" I looked around and through the horde of people, I didn't see anyone I knew. I heard my name again. "STONE!" Then this beautiful French lady approached me with the most delightful accent and said, "Stone, I'm your friend from Instagram."

Oh my God! I thought to myself. *Thank you Father. You are showing off!* I could not hold back the tears and nervous laughter. I let it go and ran towards her. She reached out her hands, I gave her mine and we embraced. She said, "You're shaking, Stone." I thought to myself, *But never my faith.* I asked, "Have we ever direct messaged before?"

"No, but I read on your Instagram post that you were coming to Paris. I hoped I would meet you." She went on as we continued to walk. "You see, Stone… I have a decision to make. I know your book is *Decision Time: How Strength Based Decision Making Changes Everything.*" I thanked her and said, "I can help you make it."

Relieved, I started walking with her, as she led the way. "I'm so glad to see you, Carnie. I'm lost." She smiled. "You're not lost in Paris. I am here." I knew God was speaking to me through her. We walked over to a café. She introduced me to her friend, Estelle. We laughed and talked about how she had been inspired by my book posts. We gave God the glory for allowing us to meet.

This was better than a made-for-Hollywood story.

Carnie retold the story twice; once in French for Estelle and again in English for me. We laughed and embraced again. Nowadays, Carnie is one of my dearest friends. God made us sister friends for life. Carnie had a dream of visiting the United States. I couldn't wait to share our divine meeting with my family. We welcomed her to our home just before the 2020 Pandemic hit.

With this end, I secretly felt accomplished. All through my trials and fears to the triumphs of my journey. You too can access your intuition. That God-given voice we *all* have within us. The one you hear that has your best interest and well-being at the center of its counsel. Not the one that encourages anger or commiserates with bad experiences.

We all have immediate access to these gifts. You have to practice being quiet, and gaining a peace of mind. You will begin to listen and start obeying your first mind. It would be a sacrilege to ignore it.

Your first mind is that calming voice ready to reassure you that the body is perishable, but the spirit is not. Yes, you will one day return to the dust from which you came. However, now is your opportunity to experience this side of the sun. So do it. Go after your dreams with confidence. Resist the lie of loneliness. You are never alone. Your divine intuition is always there.

W.O.W. - Words of Wisdom

We must develop the ability to access knowledge, wisdom and understanding. I do this by prayer, meditating on good things and quieting my mind from any thought to the contrary. Get the knowledge, seek the wisdom and pray for your understanding. The wisdom will avail itself to you. Pray for the understanding amidst your trials and tribulations. Do this when you need to make life-changing decisions. Our answers are always a thought and a prayer away.

Stone Love, Speaker, Mentor, and Author is Founder of Stoneologys Inc. She is Author of "Decision Time, Hoe Strength-Based Decision Making Changes Everything." She earned 'Presidents Club Distinction' from AT&T for outstanding sales and service, and the 'Leaders of Success Award Winner,' in recognition as one of the top three sales people in Northern California by Pacific Bell/AT&T. She is also the proud recipient of a "LIFETIME ACHIEVEMENT AWARD" from President Barack Obama's Administration in 2015, and "LIFETIME ACHIEVEMENT AWARD " from President Joseph R. Biden, Jr. Administration for 2021. Stone developed, *"The 7 Pillars To Making A Strength- Based Decision,"* a process that equips one to arrive at 'Strength-Based Decisions' every time. A graduate of City College of San Francisco, Stone is also a certified group coach with an emphasis on Neurolinguistics Programing, NLP. Stone is a wife and mother of 6 grown children and 19 grandchildren.

Turning Wounds Into Wisdom

By: Kellie Miles

* * *

In January 1999, I was a student at Community College of Philadelphia (CCP), following a two-year hiatus after high school graduation. I'm not really sure why, but I found myself enrolled in the Liberal Arts program. That's much like an undeclared major, where you explore different fields of study until you find your niche. I was a little disappointed that I didn't go to college right after high school; I felt like I missed out on campus life and all the fun that I'd heard came with it. I was 19 years old at the time and fresh out of a relationship with a guy I thought I was so in love with; I was left broken-hearted, trying to figure out college life and life in general. As I walked through the crowded cafeteria wearing my knee length yellow tank top dress suited for the hot summer weather, all these things raced through my mind.

I heard singing echoing through the noisy chatter of the café and saw a group of girls surrounding two guys competing vocally. Just being nosy, I wandered over to their area to get a closer view of what was going on. *Yup, just what I thought, two guys showing off their skills to pull in the ladies.* While I was now single and ready to mingle, I honestly didn't feel like being bothered, especially with guys that seemed to grab the attention of all the other ladies too. I was no groupie, and I was *definitely* not competing for a man's attention. I rolled my eyes and placed my tray on a free table a good distance away from them, where I could eat my lunch and catch up on my assignments in peace.

As I finished eating and gathered my things for my next class, I left the café and headed down the hallway when I heard a voice behind me. "Excuse me." I turned around and saw a friendly yet smug guy of around my age earnestly jogging over to me. His eyes were very attentive as he exclaimed how beautiful I was, asking me to give him a call as he passed me a piece of torn white paper with his phone number written on it (yes, this was before the cell phone boom). I wasn't really interested, but I was single, and he was kind of cute. I figured, *"What the heck?"* I quickly swiped his number and hurried to my next class. As I continued down the hall, I heard, "Yo, y'all was killin' it out there..." *Oh, great. Was this one of the Serenaders from the café? Ugh.* I brushed it off and focused on my destination. Slight disgust for who this guy was started to set in, slowly suffocating any interest I might have had in him at all.

Fast forward, we ended up talking, and after a while, he grew on me. Soon I felt like he could be a Band-Aid to my broken heart (or at least a rebound), and we started dating. I wasn't crazy about him, but he was cool, funny and his singing wasn't bad. I figured I'd just see how it would play out. What sustained my interest was that he was a believer in Christ and had a church home where he was actively engaged. He was so sincere about his relationship with Jesus and had so many aspirations for the things of God. I too was raised in the church; even though I didn't always live according to the instructions in the Bible, I knew God was real and that eventually I would get my life together. He being a believer was encouraging. After a few months, he proposed, and of course my crazy self said yes! I always wanted to be loved, be a wife and do the family thing. My mother was so confused and furious about our engagement. She wanted better for me and knew I could do better. At the time, I didn't see it.

Well, sure enough, the crap started to hit the fan. During our engagement, he was accused of raping three women in the music room at the college and was arrested. I didn't want to believe it and supported him through the entire trial. The story made newspaper headlines! I was working at a salon as a hairstylist, and one of the clients who sat under the dryer began reading the story aloud to her friend on the phone. She knew my then fiancé from the neighborhood. I was inexplicably embarrassed. I rushed over to her and asked if she could please keep it down because it was a disturbance to other clients. Faking as if I was grabbing hair supplies from the salon's lower level, I ran downstairs to be alone and gather myself. Just about everyone who worked in the salon knew he was my fiancé. He was later acquitted. My low self-value and desire to hold on to my idea of marriage made me stay with him.

On October 23, 1999, we got married. Yup, I was 19 years old and married my rebound nine months after meeting him, months after he faced accused rape charges. Crazy, right? My mom was livid. She couldn't stand this guy for reasons I was too blind to see. I was caught up in the idea of marriage, infatuated with the fact that he wanted to marry me. I struggled most of my teenage years with low self-esteem, self-value and feelings of incompetence. He became a barrier to hide behind when those feelings arose, so people only saw my facade. I ended up leaving my mom's church and joined his church. It was at this church that I truly gained a relationship with God and experienced Him more than I had ever at any other church before then. But that was about the only silver lining.

As time went on, I realized I was holding down a job by myself while he pursued his singing career. He had a wandering eye and disrespectfully gawked at other women RIGHT IN FRONT OF ME! We argued almost all the time, and he was verbally abusive. That band-aid was ripped right off my already wounded heart, uncovering my low self-esteem and value issues. He even pushed me to the floor of our third-floor apartment while I was pregnant with our son. When he left, I locked the door, and he broke it down in a fit of rage. I called the church, and they helped me. Thank God!

Once our son was born, he told me he couldn't wait six weeks, so he raped me while I had stitches and was recovering from labor. I didn't leave because I wanted my ideal marriage to work. Unfortunately, I was still unaware of my true value. In 2002, after leaving work at that same salon, he and I headed over to a block party. It was summer, and all our friends were there, laughing, eating good food and enjoying ourselves. Later that night, a call came through; it was his mom telling him to get home because the police were looking for him. Of course, I was confused and had so many questions. How, why, for what? When we got to the house, we were there for maybe twenty minutes when we heard the loud banging on the door. Five police officers barged in, guns drawn, yelling for him not to move. He had his shirt off and was drinking out of an orange juice carton. It was literally like a scene from the show, *COPS*.

I immediately grabbed my two-year-old son and held him in my arms, attempting to shield his face from the devastating scene. They took him outside into the squad car. I was lost as to what to do next. I grabbed my son, pressed through the angry crowd of screaming neighbors and jumped into my car to follow them to the station.

Knowing what I know now, I should have let that disgust when I first met him suffocate my interest and not made that call. But here I was, sitting at the police station with my two-year-old son who was oblivious to what was going on, crying, unable to process the trauma of it all. I listened to the charges: rape (AGAIN), indecent exposure, sexual assault, kidnapping and a few others. *Is this really happening to me right now*, I questioned. I was distraught, confused, shocked and just didn't know what the next move should be. I knew I couldn't spend the night at the jail with my two-year-old son. It was late, and there was nothing I could do at that point, so I just went back home.

I couldn't sleep at all that night with many questions running through my head. *What happened? Who is the girl? How will we get money for a lawyer? Why am I going through this again?* To calm my racing thoughts, I prayed until daybreak until finally dozing off to sleep. The next morning, still in disbelief and shock, I got up for work and prepared to take my son to childcare as if nothing was going on. After a few months, he was released on bail and yup! I was right there, still holding on to my idea of marriage. I had to be the upstanding wife, supporting her husband through the trying times of our lives. He was eventually convicted and had to serve six years in jail.

While he was in jail, my self-value began to blossom. I started developing a greater love for myself and decided not to continue with that or any other toxic relationship. I also identified the cause of my low self-value. I found that I relied more on people than I did God, and in doing so, I suffered unnecessary turmoil that could have been prevented. I began to unearth my value in God through a process of self-introspection, discovering what true love really was. Eventually I learned to trust God over man and turned my wounds into wisdom.

W.O.W. - Words of Wisdom

And the very hairs on your head are all numbered. So, don't be afraid; you are more valuable to God than a whole flock of sparrows.

— Matthew 10: 30-31 MSG

Once we realize who we are in Christ and align our perspective of personal value with His, it's likened to putting corrective lenses on the skewed vision of ourselves. Go deeper in Christ and allow Him to show you what tremendous value you have in Him.

Kellie Miles is a Playwright, Actress and Talk Show Host. She is the proprietor of Virtuous Woman Queens' Lair LLC, a women's empowerment group, Founder and President of VWQL Foundation, a 501c3 nonprofit, and host of a Christian Talk Show, The Queens' Lair. Each endeavor employs Biblical principles to enrich and empower members of the community by offering programs and resources designed to enhance personal and professional development.

A native of Philadelphia, Pa, she is a proud wife to Andre Miles, mother of a blended family of four children, and a fur baby (Onyx). In addition to her deep love for and devotion to Christ, her passions are the arts, leadership development, building and maintaining relationships, challenging thought processes to encourage mindset changes, and helping women to see their value from God's perspective.

Website: www.vwqueenslair.org
Email: info@vwqueenslair.org

Traveling Through Triumph

By: Minister JaVon Ophelia Butler

* * *

My life has truly been the definition of *traveling through triumph.* During my early childhood years, God and my mother, Joy Ann Woodland Butler, were always my guides in every decision I made for my life and career. During my journey, I learned how to wade the waters through the good and the bad.

In my family life, I was the only girl and the youngest of three. I experienced a lot of rejection when I was younger. My mother always fought to keep me on top because God had blessed me spiritually with gifts and talents. The enemy always tried to suppress my self-esteem by using people to ignore my gifts and talents. This happened from elementary school to my college years consistently with teachers, community leaders, spiritual leaders, peers and colleagues. There were seemingly people on assignment to hinder my progress and eradicate any opportunities for me to receive accolades for my scholastic and leadership abilities. My mother would always say to me, "Every knock is a boost." This is universally true for all of us. We all have experienced situations that have caused us to fail. However, we learn from those situations that "boost" us into who we are today. I used my setbacks and went on to build SeLah Productions, Inc., a nonprofit with a mission to "aspire to inspire" through productions, film and television.

In reaching our goals, we experience all types of victories, difficulties, setbacks and delays. We also experience hardships waiting for things to turn from bad to good in our lives. Even though we experience ups and downs, we are triumphant when we refuse to quit or give up. There are different steps I've used that can help you reach your goals as you journey through life. These steps have helped me to overcome and keep traveling despite roadblocks that came my way. I believe we all can benefit from these steps as we grow into our destinies.

First, we must endure the *tears* in triumph. There may have been unfair things that happened to you, unthinkable things that you could not control as a child or even as an adult. These happenings may make you cry, like me. However, cry your tears and don't stay in that place. We must free ourselves to be delivered from those experiences by facing the thoughts, moving onward to victory.

Sometimes we get *tired* of the journey towards triumph. Many days, I wanted to give up on my vision of building SeLah Productions, Inc. due to the lack of money, no destiny helpers and bad personal relationships. I would get tired of waiting on God and seeing others prosper with nothing happening on my end. In this step, you may get tired of carrying those unhappy thoughts of childhood and get exhausted from praying for something that you do not see happening, but keep believing and keep traveling. Pray and ask God for strength in your travels. God's strength is the gas to make it through the next steps in this process.

174

Next, we must get *tough* in the triumph. I had to let go of some people and things to experience my victory. Sometimes you have to make tough decisions and show tough love. Simple: let "them" or "it" go so that you can enter into your promised land.

Then, you must *transition* to triumph. God will allow you to go through transitional periods to get you to a place of destiny and purpose. Transitions can happen with relocation, health, family devastations, marriages, deaths or just life. Welcome your new thing so that you will see your triumph. My experience in this area has been the most rewarding because it was in the transition, that I began to value obedience to God. I live by this scripture: *If ye be willing and obedient, ye shall eat the good of the land (*Isaiah 1:19, KJV).

Next, we get *tested* in triumph through trials and tribulations, but we pass all of the tests through the power of God. When I lost my mother in June 2019, I thought I would die. I learned how to rise up from my bereavement. My hardships were not really about me, but for the other people that God had orchestrated for me to help along the journey. It's in this step that you take the hits of life like a good soldier and keep going until you reach your triumphal entry.

Lastly, we must exercise *tenacity* in triumph, something my mother taught me. Many times, God used her to battle on my behalf so that I got the opportunities that I rightfully deserved; whether in my academics or community service, she fought for me. Because of my mother's tenacity and toughness, I am afforded the opportunity to travel through triumph. Tenacity causes you to be determined to reach your goals in life. This will help you to rise up from the *tears,* so that when you get *tired,* you can become *tough.* You won't miss the divine and pivotal *transitions* that will help you wade through the waters of the *tests.* Tests strengthen you to have *tenacity,* leading you to completion, and then to *touchdown* in the triumph. You win!

W.O.W. - Words of Wisdom

As you continue to sojourn through the triumph, remember these Words of Wisdom: The keys of traveling through triumph will assist you in weathering life's storms and capturing life's victories. My life has been successful because I understood that despite what happens during the journey, I have the victory. If you are going to build a legacy, then you must stand until you experience triumph. There will be generations to come who will be inspired by your life. I learned to rise up out of my dark clouds so I could reach and continue to achieve my triumph for future generations. Through it all, it is comforting to know we serve a triune God that assists us through it all: Father, Son, and Holy Spirit.

Minister JaVon Ophelia Butler is Founder, Writer, Director, & Producer of SeLah Productions, Inc., (SPI), domiciled in Southeast Louisiana. She holds a B.A Degree in Political Science, with a Minor in Psychology; MPA with a Concentration on Public Policy. She is a Motivational Conference Speaker; Former President, NAACP Chapter, #6315; Member, Delta Sigma Theta, Bayou Lafourche Chapter. Min. Butler was Playwright of the Year 2017 by Church Stars Christian Entertainment Network.

She is CEO of JaVon Ophelia's ACT, (JOACT), Mentorship & Learning Program; Host, SeLah's Spot- "The Virtual View"; Chief Intercessor, SeLah's Serenity Prayer Line. She has appeared on The Word Network, Majesty Now, and NBC 33 WVLA. Min. Butler is the proud daughter of the late Joseph Butler, Sr. and the late Joy Ann Woodland Butler of Lutcher, LA, and Mother of late Westie, Jasper Orion.

YOUR LATTER WILL BE GREATER THAN YOUR PAST

By: Sherria Gross

* * *

"Until death do us part." Familiar words in vows two people say in covenant to each other in anticipation of spending the rest of their lives with each other. It is this covenant in which two hearts are bound until one breathes their last breath. However, no one told me that "death" can not only be physical, but spiritual. And when that spiritual connection is broken and expires, shriveling to dust, what is that covenant partner, the one who still yearns for a true love to do? Is it acceptable to "part" then? During my first marriage, I had to confront these questions and find the hard answers for an even harder situation.

One dark moment that I remember vividly was when I came home from my first gospel conference, in the wee hours of the morning, finding my husband laying in the street, intoxicated. From the look of things, the gawking of neighbors through windows and the perceived hushed whispers I detected in their stares, I already deducted that my neighbors had called the police. We were new to the neighborhood so of course, this was not a good look. Though I was able to drag him into the house before they arrived, I still had to answer their knocks at the door, alone, while he laid in bed. To add insult to injury, I was tasked with moving our car that he had driven to the point of completely emptying the gas tank from the middle of the street to the front of our home. I was forced to walk eight blocks, a gas container in tow to get fuel. It was 2 am. The misery of that morning stretched on once I got back and noticed my husband's phone ringing incessantly. A woman was on the other end when I answered it. Being that I was his wife, the woman he vowed to be committed to, I expected him to demand that she no longer call him. Instead, after the alcohol wore off yet again, he let me know that she could call him as much as she wanted.

I felt dismissed and humiliated. After putting me through so much stress, I wanted him to at least show that he was loyal, and he wouldn't even do that. With the memory of that night heavily weighing on my mind, I went to church the next day. I needed to be uplifted, but I just couldn't connect with the positive energy around me as I felt alone in a room full of people. No one could see the cracks in my heart or understand how weak I was becoming, despite being known as a "strong woman." It became difficult to even pray about it because my loud cries roared over the words I needed to tell Him. At this time, I believed that God wanted me to endure the pain. I thought ending my marriage would mean disappointing Him. It wasn't until I started listening to the message within my cries that I learned I was wrong. My tears were my prayers and He wanted me to acknowledge them to help me understand how my marriage was damaging my mental and spiritual health. He wanted to help me heal, not by forcing myself to stay, but finding the courage to leave.

I did eventually find that courage. And even after experiencing the relief, a long healing process was initiated. I had to heal in order to value myself. I had to heal from the severed tie of our bond. Even though it had been unbearable, I still loved him. But I had to love myself and God more. I had to face my failed marriage in the face. I had to reflect on the signs that God showed me for years that my husband was unfaithful, but ignored. I had to take a long hard look at reality.

However, I was not alone. God was with me every step of the way. He held my hand through it all, and it was His comfort that got me out of the bed some mornings when all I wanted to do was wallow in my hurt. He nursed my heart back to health, teaching me how to love by loving me first and putting me back together. A stronger me. A better me. One that was now vowing to love herself through thick and thin. The love God showed me loved me back to life. And His love was stronger than death. Even if death did part me from this life, He promised that His love would never die. I built my new life on that love and it hasn't failed me yet.

As a pastor today, I meet women going through difficult marriages. Using what I learned from my experience, I encourage them to choose the path that protects their spirit the most even if it means walking away. I know that the idea of starting a new relationship can be scary. I was 36 with three teenage kids when I became divorced and I kept wondering, *who would want to be with me now*? By letting God heal me, I invited in patience and kept my heart light to prevent any bitterness from settling. And when I eventually got remarried, I embarked on a quest to rediscover who I was. I gave myself permission to reconnect with myself.

It is also important for women to understand that we are only human at the end of the day, and it's not solely our responsibility to keep our marriages alive. Marriage is a collaboration, so it takes two to work through hardships and obstacles.

We as women must preserve our self-love and not lose ourselves in giving our all to men who may not be grateful. On top of that, finding a new love may seem impossible after a divorce. It may even seem harder to learn how to re-love yourself. But if you trust in His plan for you, then you can find your way. I was able to learn to love myself deeply and offer that fulfilled person to my now husband. I now experience a fulfilled life of loving God, people, my family and myself. My latter was greater than my past. Divorce doesn't have to be a finale; I am a living testimony. God is always opening new doors that can show you the beauty of a new beginning.

W.O.W. - Words of Wisdom

Your latter will be greater than your past / You will be blessed, more than you could ask / Despite all that has been done, the best is yet to come / ... And your latter will be greater than your past/ All things are possible.

- Lyrics from Martha Munizzi's *Your Latter Will Be Greater Than Your Past*

Like a phoenix, God wanted me to rise from the ashes and the darkness by which I felt enclosed because He knew that I deserved more. I had the fire within me all along, it just had to be illuminated again so I could embrace my power and accept that ending my marriage would not be the end of me. However, when the process got hard, I had to remain hopeful. I had to remember that God loved me, in spite of the failure that the divorce sometimes made me feel that I was. He reminded me that He had plans to prosper me and not harm me, plans to give me hope and a future (Jeremiah 29:11). I relied on His vision of love for me while I was still learning to love myself. And His love nursed me back to health. After learning to love myself, and Him, He introduced me to a healthy love with my now-husband. My life is proof that failure is never final and your latter can be greater than your past!

Sherria Gross is a devoted wife, a daughter, a mother, a grandmother, an author and an entrepreneur/CEO. She is a native of Philadelphia, PA and currently resides in New Jersey. She is a Prophet and the Pastor of a church in Philadelphia, PA.

Sherria has earned a Master's Degree in Divinity and a Bachelor Degree in Organizational Leadership. For many years she has served many communities in the mountain Education. She was privileged to service urban communities with educational goals as a Medical Assistant, Dental Assistant, Massage Therapist and various other fields. Her presence within her 21 years of the post-secondary educational system brought change to the countless lives she has encountered.

She is the host of God's Girl Prophetic Gathering where she empowers women from all walks of life. Her passion is to see women and men of God be healed, whole, delivered and set free to live life to the fullest based on their God given mandate and purpose.

Gmail:sherriaallen76@gmail.com |Facebook: @Sherria Gross | Instagram: @mrs_sgross

From Section 8 to Commercial Real Estate

By: Enasha Bradshaw

* * *

This chapter is dedicated to all the women who are READY to show up and show out. Yes, you, who has been hiding, but is tired of settling. The woman who sees the glass as neither half empty nor half full, but is READY for her cup to runneth over. The one that is READY and realizes that she is, and has, more than enough, equipped to pursue and fulfill her God-given will.

Furthermore, I dedicate this to my living legacy, my children.

My legacy started long before my birth, but it was particularly activated in 2016, when God told me to quit my job. I was on a career path and had stayed there longer than any other place of employment. I loved the company and was making more money than I had ever made. I had all the perks, but little to no time for my children—they were being raised by daycare. To top it off, I was recently separated from my now ex-husband for what started as a very complicated divorce. My only safe haven was the church, which is where I should have been the most. This job had made all accommodations for me to work through what was a stressful time in my life, so I felt indebted to it.

Not even a year in my newfound position, God's voice spoke to me as clear as if He was sitting right next to me in my cubicle. God told me to quit?! Instantly, I thought, *God, who do You want me to deliver that message to—because that surely is not for me.* God said it again, giving me an exact date a few weeks away. My parents, the bishop and pastor of my church, asked if I was sure. My friends thought I was crazy, and my boss didn't understand. But when God gives you a vision, you have to stop giving people permission to control your destiny. So, I stood on my decision to follow the will of the Lord and quit my job on the appointed day.

For my obedience, I walked into blessings with ease. I had more than enough money despite being unemployed; my cup started running over. Though I was on Section 8, they had a program that allowed me to be one of the few African Americans to live in a gated community with two pools, a playground on-site and an observatory! It was quiet and spacious. I had my own office, walk-in closets, a dish washer and more. God had spoiled me so and was preparing me for a bigger purpose. God wanted to know if He could trust me to be obedient to His will, even if it meant letting go of something I loved and had worked hard for.

Throughout the years, I had changed jobs several times to find money, perks and a schedule that allowed me to be a mom to my two beautiful children. At most jobs, I loved what I did, but hated being overworked and underpaid. The most depressing part for me was missing my children's birthdays, events and having to leave them at daycare all day. They were the first ones there, and the last ones picked up. Still, I obeyed God but within a few years I was working again at a similar job- that was until I was fired from what I thought was a *second* opportunity at my dream job! A few months

186

prior, God had spoken clearly again! He told me to start a business. Now this was something I'd never done before, had experience with, or even understood. So, I told God these two things:

1. *If You want me to start this business, then You'll have to download everything in me that I need to know.*

2. *I would do it in about two years, once I worked on the plans I have for myself.*

I am pretty sure God was laughing hysterically at that point, especially considering my favorite scripture was Jeremiah 29:11: *'For I know the plans I have for you,' declares the LORD, 'plans to prosper you and not to harm you, plans to give you hope and a future'* (Jeremiah 29:1, KJV).

Instantly, everything started going wrong at the job that I had prayed for and loved. I was warring against principalities because of my disobedience. It was wearing on my health, my mental state and I started spiraling into depression. God had to remove me from that job, or else that job was going to take me out!

Now Sis, I'm talking to you. Yes, you, the one that says I'm not qualified. The one who has analysis paralysis! The one who thinks they are not capable of such a thing as this. The one who has yet to pull the trigger and get started because of the excuses you are making. If God has called you, then Sis, God has qualified you…so go forth in Jesus' name! I thought I was not qualified to be a Credit

Specialist because at the time, I had bad credit. Unqualified in the eyes of man, but my God saw the best in me—and He sees the best in you, too! I found a business opportunity that would change my and my family's entire life, all *because* I had bad credit. I've been able to help people nationwide achieve their goals of higher credit scores, get into homes, buy cars, while helping several Realtors get more families into homes! Having an excellent credit score now, I have gone from Section 8 to OWNING Commercial Real Estate. During the pandemic, I was able to purchase a six-figure home and I was only asked to put a $700 down payment at closing! At the same time, I purchased both my first commercial property and my first rental property.

I am now a successful business owner known as the Credit Professor. I teach people the power of credit and financial literacy. I went from having five-figure years to having five-figure months. I make my own schedule and will never have to miss another moment with my children. As the cherry on top, I am now happily married to my amazing husband of four years, who also is one of my business partners. My business has become my ministry and my calling is to help people see the hope and future God has for them; to encourage them to walk in their purpose of Entrepreneurism. I live a life of not only success, but significance—doing what God called and qualified me to do. I hope you do the same, Sis!

W.O.W. - Words of Wisdom

Remember this, God does not call the qualified, but He qualifies the called.

Sister, you have been called and He will qualify you in your obedience to the Word of God. We all serve a purpose, and you must find that for which God has purposed you. God is not asking for perfection or for you to be the best in the industry. God called you to do only the part which He has given YOU! God says: **GET STARTED NOW!** You already have what it takes. Leave all doubt, worry and fear and go get your blessings from your obedience. I hope that my testimony will move you in such a way that you run after your calling, knowing that God created you with a purpose to walk into with confidence.

Enasha Bradshaw is a God-Fearing wife and mom of 2. She is an Inspirational Speaker who has successfully invested in real estate, rental and commercial property. She is known on social media as the Credit Professor. To date, she is the Co-founder and Credit Specialist of a one-stop shop called In the Moment Financial Services which host many different workshops, including but not limited to entrepreneurship, first-time homebuyers, as well as credit. She also does everything virtually for her nationwide clientele at www.inthemoment101.com.

Her mission to bring financial literacy is why she offers FREE consultations for a wide-range of financial services including Credit Restoration, LLC Formation, Tax Preparation, Bookkeeping, and Small Business Consulting to name a few. Moreover, she has mentored over 150 people nation-wide and her mission is to work closely with individuals and small businesses to produce minority entrepreneurs as well as coach them in building generational wealth.

Your Beginning Does Not Have to Be Your End

By: Annette Hampton

* * *

I came into the world launched into a world of confusion. I was born on New Year's Day in Philadelphia, Pennsylvania. Since it was New Year's Day, my dad decided to take my older siblings to the Mummers New Year's Day parade. Would you know I decided it was time for me to make an appearance? My mother was left home alone while all her children were taken to the parade. To her surprise, she went into labor and began to pray she would not deliver her child until her husband returned home. Unbeknownst to her, it was already too late. I was her fifth child so labor was swift, and my mother birthed me on the bedroom floor of our home. Although my due date was approaching, my parents were not expecting me when I decided to arrive, and that moment initiated the beginnings of my messy life. Chaos ensued once my father and siblings returned home. My father did not know if I was going to make it. After making many calls, they finally found a home doctor, but he refused to come to the house until my father put fifty dollars in his hand. This was one week after Christmas and dad had spent the last of his cash on the parade that day. My dad frantically decided to call my aunt and she paid for the doctor to come tend to both Mother and I, cutting the umbilical cord that still had me tied to her. I was named after my aunt to honor her role in coming to our rescue.

What an entrance! Life for my family just became more difficult in the years that followed. They were just as unprepared to handle family matters as they were my entrance into the world. My mom and dad struggled to maintain a peaceful relationship. They each had issues and it was not uncommon for them to end up in a physical altercation. The fighting was so bad that when my mother finally left my dad for good, the last time, I was glad. I was four years old and breathed a sigh of relief and wished she would never return to him. Why was a four-year-old baby glad her mother left home? I was a child that experienced turbulence, fear, trauma and distress all her life up until her mother's departure. It never dawned on me that my mother was gone and had left all her babies behind. I somehow intrinsically understood that it was better to have one parent in peace than two that maintained a tumultuous relationship. I was now one parent down and I knew we were no longer a complete family. My oldest sister and father provided for us from that day on.

Ironically, because of my chaotic entrance into the world, every one of my older siblings tried to shield me with their love. They carried, cuddled and loved me. This was the foundation of my love relationships with all my older siblings. They always made me feel like I was special. That gift of bonding with my siblings would cement us for the rest of our lives. A rainbow at the end of the storm. Each time I peel back the emotions during difficult times in my life, I see how God grew, provided for and protected me. He then used me to be an instrument of change and deliverance in the lives of others. No experience was wasted.

Although my early years were filled with good times with my older siblings, uncertainty, insecurity, doubt, and a lack of confidence filled my heart, resulting in a poor self-image. I began to feel less than others. Somedays I questioned my existence, but God would remind me that He saved me and had a purpose for my life.

I tried to measure up in school, but I never felt as bright as my siblings. I was sandwiched in between two amazingly intelligent siblings. To my dismay, they were highly gifted and were noticed by others. I still felt very much invisible to most, but I would prefer it that way. In my eyes, my siblings were near geniuses; I was barely average by all standards. They understood how to excel and by all accounts, I did not.

This insecurity was confirmed by my high school guidance counselor who called me in my senior year to talk about my plans. I told her I was planning to go to college because I wanted to be a teacher. The counselor served notice that I would never be "college material". There it was. It was confirmed; I was not bright enough to attend college. She suggested that the best I could do was go to secretary school to be trained as a secretary. No offence to secretaries, they have been invaluable all my life, but I honestly thought I could have been a good teacher. I went home and told my dad what the counselor said. He turned around and said, "Baby, you can be whatever you want to be. If you want to go to college, go." I decided to apply and got in, but was fearful once I enrolled; I figured

I was going to flunk out because I did not belong there. I thought my experience in college was going to be a revolving door. Why? Because inside my heart, I felt I would never succeed.

This attitude continued well into college where I experienced hard core racism for the first time in my life. I was one of two female African-American students who was a part of the freshman class. The racism experienced along with me discovering my academic preparation was far below standard, ushered me into a disheartened state. I cried before God because of the unfairness of it all. *I am with you and I will never forsake you*, He answered. *Study, apply yourself, seek help and rely on Me. I am your all sufficient One.* I attended tutorial sessions to supplement my academic deficiencies and enhance my study habits. God assured me that He had opened the door of college for many reasons, and I would experience Him like I never had in all my life. He was right. I grew closer to Him because I knew I needed Him. I began to address the racism on campus which had become a purpose of advocacy for me. I would go on to work on university campuses for over 35 years and became an advocate for students and staff who were facing questionable situations on campus.

I began working in Higher Education as an administrator not too long after I graduated from college. Higher education has been life changing for me. I took advantage of every course and training lecture I could attend. To work at a place where I could learn all the time was a God-send to me. A psychologist on campus asked if I could meet with some of his clients because he had too many

194

students reaching out to him. I said sure, and there began my love for counseling. What I discovered was God had given me the skill to counsel and aid students individually and in group settings through the counseling process of self-introspection and healing. What a powerful moment when I discovered I was naturally gifted at something! And it was only discovered by taking on new and different challenges and being open to change. My willingness to step beyond my comfort zone catapulted me into discovering my life's passion.

Counseling is now my gift to others. I went on to secure the necessary training and credentials to effectively counsel others. I have been training in this area for over thirty years now. During my tenure at various universities, part of my responsibilities was to connect university resources to the communities which surrounded the institution. There began my love for community service. My second passion. I loved working with the community, helping them to identify and secure the resources needed to promote an improved quality of life. I found this work refreshing because from my perspective I got to be involved with people from all walks of life. These folks came with a myriad of experiences, education and different outlooks on life. From veterans, community advocates and neighbors to educators, I listened and I gained wisdom.

My job in Higher Education required me to pursue a Master's degree to position myself for promotion. I received my first Master's degree and thought it was such a delight to continue to learn as I grew on my journey. I continued my academic pursuits at an Ivy League institution where I was employed. I was enrolled in my second Master's Program when those old feelings of inferiority surfaced. The fact that it was an Ivy League school brought to the forefront of my mind that most classmates I would be competing against had been attending private schools all their lives. I was sure that they had the best of everything and everyone their whole lives. The professors were the best of the best and challenged us to work toward our full potential.

I realized that my fears and feelings of mediocrity had never been dealt with, but were just pushed down into my subconscious mind. The second I tried to progress in a new area of my life, fear would rear its ugly head to hinder my progress. God challenged me at that very moment: *Face your fear! I created you for a purpose. Everything you are doing is to perfect the talents, gifts and abilities I have placed in you to help and heal folks I send your way. Do not ever let Satan, people or even you deter you from the mission I have given you. From this day forth walk in confidence, in who I have created you to be in this life.* God made it clear to me that He would use me as His tool to teach, lead and guide many into the knowledge they so desperately needed. From that day forward (and it has been many years since), God has allowed me to teach in college classrooms, workshops, seminars, classes and conferences all over the nation.

The latest challenge came during this last year when I had Covid. I entered the hospital and was placed on oxygen because my oxygen levels were too low. I had a bad case of pneumonia. I had three doctors in my room, a disease specialist, a pulmonologist and the regular doctor on call. They were trying to figure out my treatment. At that moment as I lay in the hospital bed, I realized they were not sure of what to do. I prayed: *Father, they don't know what they are doing.* The Lord said to me, *No, they don't know, but you are not in their hands. You are in My hands. Lay in the bed and rest and I will take care of you.*

He did just that. He took care of me and I recovered from Covid. God told me Covid came as the result of Satan trying to shut my mouth. Before I was diagnosed with it, I was teaching three classes, had numerous counseling clients and was doing community work. I went back to teaching harder and with more intensity than I'd ever taught before.

I am secure in God in all aspects of my life. I have allowed the Prince of Peace to rest in my soul. My present is full of faith and confidence, and I truly rely on God to direct me moment by moment. God is no respecter of persons. He is not going to do more for me than He will do for you. I am a living proof. Your beginning does not have to be your end.

- There is a lesson to be shared out of every challenge you have experienced.

- Don't ever let anyone else determine your future.

- Your turbulent past does not have to determine your future.

- Get comfortable learning and trying new things. It may help you discover your passions in life.

- Sometimes the solutions you have discovered for the problems you face will be helpful for others. The experiences you have gone through may indeed be healing medicine for others.

Dr. Annette V. Hampton has been a member of the Christian Stronghold Baptist Church for the past fifty-five years. Annette serves as the Counseling Center Director as well as the Executive Director of Alpha Community Development Corporation. Annette Is a private therapist and is an instructor for Christian Research and Development where she teaches the advanced Biblical counseling course. Annette has been a national seminar and workshop speaker for over 30 years.

Annette received her Master of Social Work Degree from the University of Pennsylvania, and her PhD. in Counseling Education and Supervision from Regent University. Annette is a Licensed Social Worker.

Philadelphia PA

Email: ahampton2@gmail.com

Facebook: https://www.facebook.com/annette.hampton.714

HER CHILDREN RISE UP AND CALL HER BLESSED

By: Kim Jacobs

I have overcome many challenges that have shaped me into the person that God purposed me to be. I place everything in His hands and trust His will for my life. My life on this earth is not about me—it is to represent Christ, to use the gifts and talents He gave me, and to teach others to overcome their circumstances. When I die, I want to hear, "Well done thy good and faithful servant, Kim. Welcome into the joy of the Lord!"

Growing up at *The Bottom* and being raised by a devoted, hard-working, single mom was pivotal in me deciding to rise up and build a legacy at an early age! I knew I was poor, but I never embraced it. My mom made me believe I could be anything. I often wondered why some people had so much while others struggled. I quickly learned that no one is better than anyone else, we all needed one another. I started my journey of leadership by being voted the senior class president in high school and then again in college at James Madison University. At the age of 18, I accepted Jesus Christ as my personal savior, and I have been winning souls for Christ ever since. Even as a believer, I have gone through some extreme seasons in my life. "To everything there is a season and a time to every purpose under the heaven (Ecclesiastes 3:1, KJV)." One difficult season in particular stands out to me.

My twelve-year-old son, Gabriel Michael Jacobs, died unexpectedly on April 9, 2015. I prayed for a different outcome and begged the physician to give him my heart, but God decided that Heaven would be his new home. When Gabe passed away over one hundred youth gave their lives to Jesus Christ at his home-going celebration. His life was not lived in vain. Gabe was affectionately known as "Guardian Gabe" by his peers and served as the anti-bullying mediator. However, his legacy lives on through me and my wonderful team of volunteers that help operate Gabe's Heart Foundation at Gabesheartfoundation.org. We get the opportunity to bless complete strangers by "Doing it Gabe's Way: Random Acts of Kindness." Gabe's passing also inspired me to create The Mother Dreamer Movement to encourage mothers with dreams and goals, helping them pursue them while raising their children. The City of Charlotte has even designated August 10th as a day to remember Gabriel Michael Jacobs. Just like Gabe, we don't know how long we have on this earth to impact others. People need you now!

Another pivotal moment in my life is when I witnessed my daddy pass away in front of me at 71. He focused on serving the underprivileged, and was known as "The People's Bishop!" He wanted people to hear God's Word so badly that he would place his church speakers outside the building while he preached from inside. I witnessed hundreds of people sitting outside on buckets and on their porches, hearing him preach God's Word even though they never entered the building. That's legacy building. The city of Palatka designated May 7th to honor him.

Proverbs 31:28, KJV states: "Her children arise up, and call her blessed; her husband also, and he praiseth her." Just like those around me who have passed, I want to make a difference and be called blessed. I am determined to use every gift God has given me to help others realize that no matter what they experience in life, God can bring them out. I am currently the host of The Kim Jacobs Show and I have a great team that secures our featured guests. They share their backstories of what they overcame to become who they are today. We are living our motto, "Bringing Balance to the World One Household at a Time."

My children are five human beings who love me on a level no one else will ever completely and unconditionally understand. I was told by a surgeon that I couldn't have children, but God had a different plan. I thank God He allowed me and Frank to have a union that produced the greatest blessings in my life. I asked my children what my legacy is in their eyes. This is what each of them had to say:

Frank Jr., 24 years old student at UNC Chapel Hill and an E-Commerce expert, said:

> *Mom, your legacy is to treat others the way you want to be treated. You exemplify that! People are usually too self-centered to do that. You taught me that it never hurts to be a good person. Without you, I wouldn't be the person that I am today. I have never seen anyone else willing to do this for strangers and friends alike—all without expecting anything*

in return. We often forget about those who are selfless and inspiring because they make it look easy. Your values and hard work have set an example for me to follow. Mom, if I were to give you a rating on a scale, it would be 10 out of 10. You have taught me the value of self-education, reading and the value of believing in myself. I enjoy learning, reading and bettering myself because of you. I love you, Mom! The person that I am today, literally and figuratively, is all because of you!

Ivan, 20 years old and a student at UNC Charlotte, said:

Mom, you have a generous nature. You and Gabriel, before he died, shared the same trait of being kind to everybody. Even if it puts you in a bad situation by being so open to everybody, you still do it anyway. Your kindness extends beyond the person you are helping. I never shared this with you before, but I will tell you now since it was because of your impact on me that I decided to do this. When I was in high school, I decided to make friends with people other students would consider "weird." Through these friendships, I learned that "normalcy" is a state of mind and that kindness is more important. In my opinion, there is no normal or weird in life, just kindness. I can see your legacy through how you have raised us. There is a noticeable and dramatic difference in how you raised us versus some other families. My siblings are more mature than some adults based on my observation. Mom, I could be doing anything I want and so could my siblings, but because of how you raised us we choose the right thing. You gave me a good head start in life, and I am going to pass this kindness to others.

Jeremiah, 16 years old aspiring actor and student at Northwest School of the Arts, said:

Mom, you show me how being a nice person can really pay off and genuinely change someone's life. I have watched you just speak to a cashier and it changed the person's whole demeanor. I watch you go get bread every week to feed the homeless, people working at the post office, car wash, and everywhere in the community. I see how happy it makes people to know that someone is thinking of them when they don't have to do that. Even the Great Harvest Bread Company (donor) looks forward to your arrival. Seeing how much better others are from your actions every week helps me be a nicer person too. Mom, your legacy is forgiving people and not holding grudges. I love you, Mom, and I thank you for teaching me at an early age how I should treat my wife and children in the future.

Jayla, 13 years old, an honor student at Guardian Gabe Academy who enjoys gardening and animating on YouTube, said:

I learned how to be an amazing and kind person because of who you are, Mom. You taught me to greet people with a smile or wave; with love every time, even if they don't show the same kindness in return. You taught me how to be a good person in general. You taught me to pray for people so they don't have to face hell. You pray with me, and you make me feel like I can do anything, Mom. Thank you for that. I am just a better person because of all that you do for me, Mom.

Gabriel, 12 years old at the time of his passing and an honor student/football player/anti-bullying mediator, often said:

Mom, I hug and kiss you every day because I want you to feel my love. I love you so much, Mom! I like when we do family dates and go to eat and go to the movies. I think we should do this every week as a family tradition. I want us to travel the world together as a family. We will when I go to the NFL. Mom, I get my kindness from you and that is why I got the Christianship award on my teams! Hearing these words from my children confirms that my legacy will live on. As you build your own legacy, here are some of my personal tips for you:

- Identify the names of specific people that you will train and mentor to carry the torch after you pass away.
- Have Accountability Family Meetings—let each person in your family share resources to help one another.

- We all have the same 24 hours, so let God lead you to prioritize and maximize your day.
- When something is not working, make immediate adjustments.
- Stop second guessing yourself—you are the only one holding yourself back! God already believes in you.
- Do something! Stop waiting for the perfect time.

And we know that all things work together for good to them that love God, to them who are the called according to his purpose. What shall we then say to these things? If God be for us, who can be against us?

- **Romans 8:28-31, NIV**

God believes in us and He trusts us with the gifts that He has given to us. Use them! God is for us! He is our everything! Everything that we experience will somehow work out for our good.

As Les Brown says, "Make a conscious decision today to *live full and die empty!"*

Kim Jacobs, affectionately known as The Balance Doctor, is host of The Kim Jacobs Show. She is the daughter of the late Bishop Elijah Jackson and Ella Spratley. Raised by her single mother, Kim believes that women can succeed regardless of life's circumstances. She accepted Christ at 18 years old. She received her B.S. degree from James Madison University and an MBA from Southeastern University. In addition to being a wife and mother (Frank Jr., Ivan, Gabriel, Jeremiah, and Jayla), Kim is a Certified Seminar Speaker (Les Brown's Network), and an Entrepreneur. Kim created The Mother Dreamer Movement to inspire mothers to raise powerful children while pursuing their dreams. Kim is the founder of Gabe's Heart Foundation (gabesheartfoundation.org), which honors her 12-year- old son (Gabriel) who passed away unexpectedly. She ensures that he is smiling from Heaven by "Doing it Gabe's Way" Random Acts of Kindness.

The Forgotten Ingredient

By: Dr. Juliet McBride

But the Comforter, which is the Holy Ghost, whom the Father will send in my name, he shall teach you all things, and bring all things to your remembrance, whatsoever I have said unto you. Peace I leave with you, my peace I give unto you: not as the world giveth, give I unto you. Let not your heart be troubled, neither let it be afraid.

— John 14:26-27, KJV

Jesus spoke these words to His disciples before His departure to the Father, words of comfort and peace. This scripture has been a constant compass and guide for my life. As a child and young adult, my maternal grandmother, Grandma Anna, impressed that scripture on my heart and mind. Anytime, I've had to make a decision that would change the trajectory of my life, she would ask me, "What did the Lord say?" or "Did you pray about it?" When I was accepted to the Barbizon Modeling School in New York City, I ran to Grandma Anna in uncontrollable excitement, waving the acceptance letter. She waited until I finished reading the letter and asked me one question: "What did the Lord tell you to do?" It was during those critical times in my life as a young adult that I began to build a relationship with the Lord. That relationship taught me to trust the leading of the Holy Spirit throughout my life into adulthood.

Years later, I was making a familiar dish for my family, and put all of the ingredients in a bowl with anticipation to serve and eat. Once my family sat at the dinner table, one of my sons winced after his first spoonful. As politely as he could, he mentioned that my dish did not taste the same. My husband and the rest of the family agreed. I sat rehearsing in my mind, every step of the recipe. I tasted it myself and it *did* taste different, but why? What was the missing ingredient? What did I forget to add to this amazing dish? How could I forget an ingredient for a dish that I had cooked many times before? Truth was, I became so comfortable with making the dish that I felt I had it under control without looking at the recipe.

Unfortunately, leaning on my own understanding, I had forgotten the main ingredient. If I had checked the recipe in the cookbook, I would have been reminded of all of the ingredients, but I neglected to do so. I would have saved myself emotional stress, embarrassment, frustration and wasted time. Likewise, we must be careful of thinking, we have everything under control spiritually in daily situations. Sound familiar? With expressions like *I got this*, *I'm a boss* and *I'm straight!,* we journey in life with this type of attitude, making mistakes that could be avoided. Are your plans God's purpose? Just take a moment and think. In the Bible, which is our *recipe* book, Proverbs 3:5-6, KJV states; *Trust in the Lord with all thine heart; and lean not unto thine own understanding. In all thy ways acknowledge Him, and he shall direct thy paths.*

There are many ingredients we need in order to have a fruitful and abundant life. Love, peace, salvation, prayer, study of the Word of God, fasting and fellowship with other believers are a few. But the "missing ingredient" that has become obsolete for many Christians is the invitation of the Holy Spirit in their daily lives. Many do not allow the Holy Spirit to guide their decision making. Then they blame God when situations fall flat. We must trust the Lord in ALL life decisions. He is our anchor, Savior, Redeemer and Father-God who give good gifts to His children. Furthermore, we do not know the plans God has for our lives, so we should not lean on our understanding (Proverbs 3:5). Acknowledging the Holy Spirit invites God's divine guidance. The definition of acknowledgement is the acceptance of truth that something exists!! WOW! Do you accept that the Holy Spirit exists? Truly ponder that before answering.

Picture a scene where you are sitting amongst a group of people, and someone approaches the group, acknowledges everyone by name, but does not acknowledge *you* and walks away. Everyone else in the group also notices that the greeter did not acknowledge you. You might comment under your breath that that type of behavior is hurtful and disrespectful, but unfortunately we do the same thing to the Holy Spirit. When a life situation arises, what or whom do we seek first? The first thing or person we run to is what or whom we trust most. Remember, the Holy Spirit is given as a gift from Father God. The Holy Spirit desires to commune, guide, teach and direct you. He knows the heart and mind of God for your life. Romans 8:27-28, KJV states, *And he that searched the hearts knoweth the mind of the Spirit, because he maketh intercession for the saints according to the will of God.* The Holy Spirit is not going to do the opposite of God's Word or divine directives.

Note this: because the Holy Spirit knows the will of God concerning your life, it is vital that you acknowledge Him in everything you do. When this shift happens, holiness and righteousness become more prevalent in your daily walk and journey with God. The sovereignty of God becomes the mosaic of your life; the eyes of your understanding and comprehension are maximized. When this mindset is nurtured by the Holy Spirit, Romans 8:28, KJV becomes a reality: *And we know that all things work together for good to them that love God, to them who are called according to his purpose.*

Everything that happens in your life has been orchestrated, planned, arranged and put together before the foundations of the world. Before God declared, let there be light, put the stars in the sky and formed the firmament, He had you in mind. Ephesians 1:4, KJV states: *As he hath chosen us in him before the foundation of the world, that we should be holy and without blame before him in love.*

We all have seen, experienced personally and observed others that have made decisions in which we knew the Holy Spirit was not involved. As a pastor and advisor for 40 years, I have counseled countless women that've made decisions without consulting the Holy Spirit in prayer. These decisions involved "seeking" the majority vote of others and receiving counsel from unbelievers which in turn, created confusion and spiritual blindness. These dangerous methods have caused heartache, misery, agony and distress. Many have paid a dear price that have caused emotional breakdowns, financial hardship, and trauma to their families, broken relationships, damaged ministries and diminished livelihoods.

I could write about the many trials, tribulations, triumphs, accolades, recognitions and educational achievements I've achieved, but it would have only given you a false perspective of my own personal strength. Everything I have accomplished in life has been through the guidance and empowerment of the Holy Spirit. Remember next time, before you start using the "recipe of life", don't "forget" the most essential ingredient: the Holy Spirit. Enjoy life!!!

W.O.W. - Words of Wisdom

Women don't need to find their voice. They need to feel empowered to use it and people need to be encouraged to listen.

— Meghan Markle

As I grew into womanhood, I learned to see myself through the lens of the Holy Spirit; this changed my perception of who I am in Christ. It was the study of the Word of God that illuminated my mindset. I never wanted to stand before people and preach the gospel. I felt my "voice" was only to be heard on a one-on-one basis or behind closed doors. I had to come to the realization that my "voice" was created to be heard publicly and globally, for me to give back and help others. The Bible says in Proverbs 18:21, KJV *that death and life are in the power of the tongue: and they that love it shall eat the fruit thereof.* Choose this day to give life with your voice!

Dr. Juliet S. McBride is Co-Founder of McBride Ministries, and founder of Sister Talk. Sister Talk, a networking and outreach ministry which encourages women of all ethnicities and professional backgrounds to discover their God-given purpose and talents. She sits on the Board of Ruth Sisters Fellowship International and many other humanitarian organizations. She has a B.A. in Psychology, a Master's degree in Bilingual Education and English as a New Language, and a Doctor of Divinity.

A member of The National Honor Society of Psi Chi in Psychology and The National Society of Morani Shujaa in African Studies, she is also a member of The Children's Tumor Foundation of NYC. Dr. McBride is a loving mother of three adult sons, one daughter-in-law and a grandmother of four.

Resilience Rising

By: Louisa Kiem

* * *

My story begins in the Philippines. If it wasn't for God's grace and my resilience, it would have ended there. Though I experienced a childhood like everyone does, I never felt like a child. My father's abuse caused my mother to be suicidal, so instead of playing outside, I spent my time making sure she saw another sunrise. Being the oldest of five siblings, I felt obligated to take on that responsibility. My father was also addicted to gambling and his addiction led us to poverty. To afford to attend a good private high school, I got a job at the church. Being there did bring me some peace, but that soon faded once I returned to my torn home.

I hated him. He was my father and I hated him. Deep down I really didn't want to feel that way, to see red in my mind when I thought of him. It was just so hard to love him when he constantly threw his rage at us, as if we were a group of strangers. When it came to my mom, she became abusive too. I can't say that I've ever felt love from my mom, but when she started taking out her pain on me, my heart bruised even more. No matter how much love I shared, the gap between us became deeper and deeper. If I wanted to survive, I had to leave them behind.

So at sixteen, I got married and thought love is what I needed most, my marriage was not about love at all. It was an escape at least, I wanted it to be. The brutal cycle of abuse continued with my abusive husband. We ended up having three children together and I realized it was time to get out of this marriage. Using all the courage I could find within, I finally left him in 1983 to come to America with my children. I was in my 30's when I immigrated. Once again, I had to start fresh, but this time, I found a purpose and true love.

Since I am too familiar with how it feels to not be held and protected, I decided that I wanted to be a nurse so I could give people the care and support they deserve. After five years in America, I got my degree and started working at the University of San Francisco in the transplant unit. I worked there for 20 years and then retired at 56. Currently, I help mentally ill patients at the hospital. I have a loving husband who is a Christian. We don't have any children together, but he embraces my three children and five grandchildren as though they are his own.

Although my journey was rough, I would be sugar-coating things if I said that everything was easy for me today. The abuse I experienced does impact how I respond to my family at times. Sometimes I can come off very defensive. As a nurse I work a lot, sometimes double shifts. I love my career and I am very dedicated to my work. My commute is far from home. I often sleep in my car to avoid being late for my 16-hour shift, which can put a huge strain on my family.

Regretfully, I was not able to get full closure with my mother whom I brought with me to America. My mom died in 2012 from lung cancer. Maybe we just didn't have enough time, or I just didn't have the right words to express how I felt. I'm still working on forgiving not just of my mom, but everyone who has ever hurt me so I can finally be free of all the hurt, disappointment and anger which has caused me to be bitter. I don't want my dark moments to define and overshadow the bright future God is giving me the will to build. I want to break the cycle that robbed me of my innocence so I can be a strong mother and wife. I know I must learn how to show love because I have never felt love before, until receiving Christ in my life.

For those who can relate to my story, I want you to know that we are survivors. Being a survivor comes with good days and bad days. Through it all God is able and it is important to remember that you are not alone. God is always walking alongside you, acknowledging your pain. When old memories replay in your head or maybe in your dreams, let your tears out and allow God to comfort you and guide you through it. Healing is a process so don't feel like you have to be okay all the time or put on a fake smile. Brighter days will come, and you will discover the great things that will fulfill your purpose and your need for love. We must take it one day at a time because our stories are far from over.

W.O.W. - Words of Wisdom

I can do all things through Christ who strengthens me

– Philippians 4:13, NIV

Throughout my struggles, God has been there to keep me focused and persistent. I am thankful for the strength he has given me to keep going even when my steps forward felt like a push back to the sadness I've become accustomed to. With his wisdom and spirit, I can keep making the most out of my life and fully accept that I am more than a victim, through my trials I triumph. I AM A SURVIVOR. And I am "Resilience Rising."

Louisa Kiem is originally from the Philippines. She came to the USA in 1984 and met her husband in San Francisco. They have been married for over 36 years. She has been blessed with three children and five grandchildren. Louisa have been a registered nurse for 31 years. She has worked at the University California San Francisco (UCSF) for 20 years in the Kidney, Pancreas and liver Transplant unit. She retired after 20 years of service.

Louisa is very passionate about her patients and has cried tears of joy and sadness with many of them over the years. Louisa Kiem's career has led her down a very rewarding path in life.

Currently, she works for an Adult Mental Health unit as a psychiatric nurse.

Giving Up is Not an Option

By: Dr. Tracy Johnson

* * *

Raised in Philadelphia, Pennsylvania by a single mother, I was raised as the youngest of three children. I had an older brother and sister by my mother, and three older brothers from my father. As a young girl, I was happy, loving and kind. In fact, my mother would often say, "Tracy taught me how to love and hug." It was not until the sixth grade when life changed for the worst. In the third, fourth and fifth grades, I struggled severely with reading, writing and math. In one instance, I remember being pulled out of class and taken to another room for testing. At the time, I was unaware of what was going on, but it wasn't until weeks later, when my mother accompanied me to school for a meeting that I discovered my life was going to change forever.

I was placed in special education classes, and my former peers never ceased to remind me. I was terrified and to make matters worse, I was tormented and teased every time I went to school. I would remain in special education classes throughout elementary, middle and high school. The test never identified what type of learning disability I had; it just stated that I was slow in all areas of learning: reading, writing and math. I struggled even in the special education classes. I was labeled "slow" by teachers and peers. A high school special education teacher once told my entire class that none of us could get a college education. My dyslexia, a learning disorder, affected my ability to read and write, and was not diagnosed until I became an adult.

One school counselor told me that I should give up. Giving up was never an option. I found a tutor to help strengthen my reading and writing skills using the Wilson Reading Program that employed multisensory instruction. Because of my strong faith, mentors, family and friends, I was eventually accepted at Harcum College, obtaining an Associate's degree with a 4.0 GPA. I went on to receive a Bachelor of Science from Cabrini College, graduating with high honors.

I began to turn my challenges into victories. I overcame poverty despite little support. I had been dismissed, but I was certainly not defeated. I worked for years as a custodian, cleaning school buildings for the Philadelphia School District. Although I was grateful for the consistent employment, I knew I had more to offer and that I could be more. It seemed that everyone around me focused on my limitations and not my potential.

Today, I speak as a lecturer at colleges much like the ones from which I was told that I would not graduate. I am an advocate for people with learning disabilities, particularly dyslexia. I also received an MA in Multicultural Education from Eastern University and an Honorary Doctorate of Science in Ministry from the Accredited School of Christian Ministry, Inc., affiliated with Lancaster Bible College.

I am the Founder and President of Vessels of Hope, a mentoring and networking organization for minority people with learning disabilities. I have been blessed to share my personal journey of academic achievement with inspired individuals with dyslexia and other learning disabilities, their parents and educators, as well as legislators and civic and business leaders. I was featured in the highly touted HBO documentary film *Journey into Dyslexia: Great Minds Think Differently,* released in 2011.

Throughout all of my experiences, there was one life event that had a pivoting effect on my life. It happened on the day I met my biological father for the first time when I was 20. Not having a father growing up was not uncommon in my neighborhood. In fact, most of my friends rarely spoke of having a father in the house. Although we did not talk about it much, I still experienced a void and longing that I couldn't explain.

Throughout my childhood, all of my questions about who my father was and what he looked like were usually met with vague and inconsistent responses. Growing up, I never stopped thinking about this mystery man, but I gradually stopped asking my mother questions about him. In all fairness to her, my mother made a wonderful attempt at being both mother and father to my siblings and me, yet that did little to eliminate the feeling of emptiness that haunted my childhood.

One day, everything changed. I was in my early twenties at the time, and I saw a television commercial about how to trace long-lost loved ones. The emotions regarding my father's absence surfaced again. The next day I called the organization, only to be discouraged, finding that my information about him was too scanty for them to legitimize a search. A few months passed, and I tried to forget about finding him, but it was futile. I was obsessed at that point. I was talking with my godmother on the phone one morning about my desire to find my father, and she volunteered information about who he was. "I'm surprised you didn't know the truth," she said. I was shocked at what she'd told me about his upbringing, and where he lived when he was a teenager. Armed with this knowledge, I decided to become my own private investigator.

I called a few people from my old neighborhood. I met one man who not only knew who my father was, but was a close friend of his. I didn't know it at the time, but he had just been talking with my father on the phone. The very next day, I received a phone call… from my father. When I heard his voice for the first time, my heart dropped into the pit of my stomach. After talking for a while, we agreed to meet later that day somewhere in North Philadelphia.

With a feeling of trepidation, I arrived thirty minutes early. Butterflies danced in my stomach. I had an image in my head of what he looked like, that we would have the same eyes and smile. I kept checking my watch. Then I saw a very tall African American man walking toward me. He held a long-stemmed rose in his right hand. "Are you Tracy?" he asked. I replied in the affirmative. He asked to see a picture of my mother. I handed him a picture I'd taken of my mother last summer. His eyes softened. Once he confirmed that I was indeed his daughter, he gave me an enormous hug. At that instant, that nagging void left and I felt peace.

Since that meeting, I have gained a whole new family. I have a wonderful stepmother who loves me as she would her own daughter, three stepbrothers and a host of nieces, nephews, aunts, uncles and cousins, all of whom I have become very fond of. We spend holidays together, and they support my educational endeavors. My newfound relationship with my father has changed my life significantly because I have discovered the part of myself that was missing, and I now feel loved and accepted. My dad and I knew that we could not make up for the lost years, so we resolved to make the best of the years ahead.

As it later turned out, my father had not only been missing from my life physically, but was also the "missing link" to my educational struggles. You see, my father also had dyslexia. All of my life growing up, my older sister and brother never struggled with academic challenges like I did. My father told me that he had struggled with reading and spelling in school and how difficult it was for him growing up. After my father and I got to know each other better, he became one of my best friends. I now had someone to talk to about my dyslexia; he was the only one in my family who really understood how I felt.

What I love most about my dad was his encouragement on those "dyslexic days," or days when I simply didn't seem to be able to read or spell anything right. I could always count on my dad to say, "Baby girl, you can do it," or, "I have dyslexia too, but that didn't stop me from being a sergeant in the army!" At other times he would say, "Don't ever let anyone tell you that you can't do anything because you have dyslexia." My father unfortunately passed away on April 28, 2010. While I truly miss my dad for so many reasons, I miss him the most on those really bad dyslexic days when I would count on him for an encouraging word to keep me going. What made it all so special was that it came from one heart to another!

W.O.W. - Words of Wisdom

Never, never, never give up.

-     Winston Churchill

Life has taught me to try and try again. Without perseverance, I would have never overcome the negative stigmas that were spoken over my life. Without persistence, I would have never had the opportunity to meet my father and have a great relationship with him before he passed. Don't let discouragement quench your dreams; giving up is not an option!

Dedicated to My Dad,

Sergeant Alexander (Tony) Sheed

Dr. Tracy Johnson is the Founding President and CEO of Vessels of Hope, a non-profit organization that helps individuals with learning disabilities. She is also an Adjunct Professor at Harcum College and an Enrollment Counselor at Eastern University. She has an Associate's degree in Liberal Studies, a B.A Psychology, an M.A Multicultural Education, and a Doctorate in Ministry Science. Diagnosed with dyslexia, and placed in special education classes in the sixth grade, hers is a story of perseverance, and the willingness to work harder than other students.

Tracy is the first to admit that persevering in the face of negative feedback and advice from others is very difficult. Tracy's faith and encouragement to other students with dyslexia helped to sustain her when she became discouraged over the course of her education. Tracy is a dedicated role model and a leader in the dyslexia community and other populations with learning disabilities.

AUDACIOUS CONFIDENCE

By: Alicia Couri

* * *

Audacious Confidence™ is the unshakeable belief in yourself that's so bold, so brave that you dare to step into what's possible despite your feelings, fears or failures. It means walking boldly in the direction of your dreams without limitations.

That wasn't always the case for me. I struggled with my self-confidence, worth and value. Growing up, I believed that you were either born with confidence or you weren't. If you had it, you had it—and if you didn't, well, that meant you were relegated to life on the sidelines. You'd go to school, get a job, get married, have kids and live your life as a spectator to those with extraordinary talents. You'd never step outside of your own comfort zone and be a world changer or create a legacy beyond your existence because that's not what you were born to do. Don't get me wrong, there's nothing horrible about staying in your comfort zone... unless, you have a burning desire to create something greater than yourself and you are allowing your FEARS to stop you.

My trouble was that I didn't really have the confidence to step outside of myself and go after what I saw as impossible. I had a burning internal desire to achieve great things, but I believed I was devoid of the recognizable talents that would get me there. I couldn't sing or dance; I wasn't skilled; I couldn't do anything that I saw others like Michael Jackson or Prince accomplish. I wasn't tall, or a beautiful supermodel like Naomi Campbell or Cindy Crawford, and I wasn't a great inventor like Steve Jobs. I was just plain ole me: a short, nondescript little black girl from Trinidad who spent part of her childhood in Brisbane, Australia. I didn't see myself as anything, let alone anything *special*. All I had was a deep desire to do something bigger than myself. A desire buried because I felt unworthy of having such lofty dreams and ambitions.

So where did Audacious Confidence even come from? It was a process, and it was only set in motion once I began to step out from behind my fears. Only then, was I able to see how much confidence I lacked and how many limiting beliefs were strangling my potential for greatness. It wasn't that I completely lacked confidence; I just didn't believe it was possible for me. In retrospect, moments of boldness did surface throughout my life. I did take risks as a young adult when I really wanted something. I would step out and go for it despite the naysayers. What I was missing was a sustained level of confidence.

I'm reminded of the account of the prophet Elijah in 1 Kings 18, when he stepped out with tremendous boldness and called down the fire of God from Heaven. It was so hot that it burned up the sacrifice, wood and water in the trenches and then slew 450 of the false god Baal's prophets. What was astonishing was what came after that tremendous display of power and might from the prophet. In the next chapter, we see Elijah running from Jezebel and hiding in the wilderness, afraid of what she would do to him. I liken my confidence to that—I would step out boldly to do something and then retreat under a thick veil of imposter syndrome, not believing that I was worthy of the opportunity that I just gained.

Confidence is a never-ending process. I could recount story after story of these Elijah/Jezebel moments, but what I really want to share is how I *recognized* them, and the first step I took and *still take* to keep myself from repeating them. I've found that there are seven steps in this process that have helped me accomplish things I'd never thought I could.

One of the biggest things I've had to recognize is my own value. My first real business was AC Beauty, an on-site makeup and hair service for weddings, special occasions and red-carpet events. I was doing fine, firmly planted in the mediocre zone. It wasn't great, but I would have one or two bookings most weekends from November to May, which, in Florida, is the height of wedding and event season. The summers were mostly dead. I was in search of a way to expand my business and felt taking a course in branding was what I needed. I wanted to have a stronger business brand to attract higher paying clients. I was tired of bargaining with people who didn't value my service and were constantly beating me down on my prices.

There I was, my first time ever paying for a coaching program, and I was finding it hard to drop $1,000 on an eight-week course on branding (I didn't yet understand investing in yourself and your business). What I didn't realize was, this was not a business branding course. Rather, this was helping me develop a personal brand. That was the beginning of my awakening. One of my primary limiting beliefs was that I was a "behind the scenes" person; that I belonged in the back. My coach challenged me on that one. By the end of that eight-week course, I was hooked. Since then, I am a firm believer in investing in my personal and business development, both have helped me see clearly when and how I put up barriers to my own success. Barriers that at times, have kept me from stepping out in Audacious Confidence.

As I started to attract the type of client and income that I desired, I had an epiphany: Those clients that I attracted, that constantly haggled my already too low prices were directly tied to my own self-worth. Even though it enraged me to do so, I would lower my prices every single time I heard someone's sob story about money. I realized I was prioritizing them over me, valuing their needs over mine—deep down, I didn't believe I deserved more. I relegated myself to a mediocre life and thought I should be thankful for what I was being paid. I finally reached a point where I was fed up and said, "No more!" My prices were my prices, and I deserved to get paid for what I did because I brought more to the table than just beautiful makeup and gorgeous hair. I gave my clients confidence and self-assurance as I ushered in an atmosphere of peace in their presence. I was helping others see the beauty that radiated beyond just that one moment in time. I was skilled and fast—I got them ready on-time and never cut corners.

In addition, in order to really know and understand myself better, I took multiple assessments to help me uncover my strengths and blind spots. One of the most powerful for me was the Kolbe Assessment, and it is why I later became a certified consultant. Trust me, understanding yourself and loving yourself is the #1 key to building your Audacious Confidence.

I have grown in my confidence journey to know that there is no such thing as being born into the Confidence *Haves* or *Have Nots*. You can have the life you dream and go after your life and purpose with determination of mind and confidence, audacious to be exact!

Beloved I pray above all things that you prosper and be in health even as your soul prospers.

– 3 John 2, NLT

This is God's will for your life. He wishes for you to prosper, be in good health and operate in a state of peace and wellness in the city of your soul. Beloved, this is our legacy, gifted to us by God Himself. Who are we *not* to be prosperous, healthy and well in our soul if the Almighty God of the Universe has claimed this heritage for our lives before our existence?

A former Mrs. Elite United States Woman of Achievement 2020. Alicia Couri has expanded her multiple talents to influence, educate, inspire and entertain audiences as an Audacious Confidence™ Growth Expert. As the RedCarpetCEO™, she produces and hosts a nationally syndicated Podcast, "Leading with Audacious Confidence", and a live web show, "Small Business Saturday Shout-Out." Alicia is an author, dynamic speaker and actor who shares incredible messages on overcoming low self-esteem and lack of self-confidence.

Alicia Couri Inc. is a boutique consulting firm that offers Strategic Talent Solutions to help High-Level Executives run audaciously proactive teams. Alicia has featured on many network TV shows, radio and podcasts sharing beauty and style tips that are also found in her books, "Your Signature Style: Unlocking The Confidence Style &/Influence of the Savvy CEO," and "Age with Audacious Confidence: 21+ Tips to Look and Feel Younger."

Story of Hope Life After Loss

By: Christine Hotchkiss

* * *

In this thing we call life, there are many things we either do not understand or take for granted until something stops us in our tracks and changes our new *norm*. We have heard many times how life is not meant to be difficult and yet, we come across difficulty often. This difficulty also includes having no answers to life's pertinent questions. I'm not talking about the age-old questions of what *is the purpose of life?* But the inquiries to which we may never have answers. Those mysteries that cause us to observe a new perspective with a changed heart. Let me share my journey.

March 28, 1989. I became a mother at the age of 19, barely understanding life myself. On this day, my daughter Nicole Marie was born, one of many days that my life was forever changed. Nicole was my everything. I never knew how much another individual could mean to me until I became her mother. She was the first granddaughter for both sides of the family and was the apple of everyone's eyes. She was so full of life and giggles; she hardly cried and always excelled in everything she did. The joy of watching her grow and become her own person was one in which I took pride. Six years later, my son Austin was born. This too was a surprise because I did not come from a family of boys and my children's father was the youngest and only boy in his family. I remember for a split second asking myself how I was going to love them both, one being

236

a boy and one a girl. It did not take long for me to realize both Nicole and Austin were individuals and yes, boys are different than girls, but the reality was they were both my everything. I was grateful and blessed beyond belief. Being a parent to a boy and a girl was truly a gift.

The years went on and Nicole and Austin were remarkably close to one another. Nicole was always there for Austin as a big sister should be. And Austin being the little brother that either irritated Nicole or showed her how special little brothers are, was there for her. Fast forward as Nicole and Austin grew older, they were involved in more activities to keep them busy or help them grow. Each of them was successful in their own way. Nicole was the outgoing extravert and involved in anything she could do in her school or neighborhood. Austin enjoyed dabbling with jumping his bike, skateboarding, remote control cars and trying to play sports. The one thing we all agreed on as a family was being active, enjoying travel and the outdoors. As a family, we loved going to the California Sand Dunes and riding our ATV's, four wheeling wherever there was a hill, mountain or terrain to ride open and free. These are the times Nicole and Austin became competitive with one another on who could ride the fastest or get the dirtiest. Still, Austin was always about the wheelies. Ah, boys will be boys. For many years we would go to the California Sand Dunes for the two-week winter break when the kids were out of school. In those last two weeks of December, we would also celebrate Austin's birthday on the 30th. It was extra fun for us to celebrate the winter break and his birthday, doing what we all loved.

December 2006 was the last year my life was to be "normal" as I had known it to be. That year was the last family trip I would remember as we were. As usual, we had set up camp as hundreds of other dunners did for two weeks. Dust and sand everywhere, campfire set up, firewood stacked, coolers stacked outside, tables set up with snacks and the sand toys parked. This place became a city all in itself with all the campers and off-road toys everywhere. One big sandbox of fun.

Nicole and Austin loved racing one another up the hills and racing their dad on the straight away. On December 30th, we celebrated Austin's 11th birthday with Nicole making him a cake, as she always loved making her brother feel special. We spent the next day and a half enjoying the dessert and doing what we loved. On the evening of December 31st, New Year's Eve, as a family we decided to take our 4x4 truck and go watch the races that would take place nightly at the top of the dunes, otherwise referred to as Competition Hill. We had done this many times before, but little did we know, this was going to be the last time. Climbing out of our truck, we proceeded to the path. In our attempt we had come to a peak of a dune that we did not expect, and rather than being able to back down the way we came up, we found our vehicle being sucked in by the sand forcing our truck to roll out of control down the other side of the dune. The sand and water were not forgiving and there was no traction to grab ahold of the earth's surface. As our vehicle continued to flip over and over, Nicole was seated in a window seat and was ejected. Unfortunately, because of her injuries she did not survive, passing away on New Year's Day 2007.

Another new chapter of my life began with no answers, and lots of pain that I have had to work through. My family broke up and the pieces that remained left me to figure out how to live a new *norm*. There were years I felt I was sitting on a block wall between the celebration of my son's birthday, December 30th and New Year's Day, now being a new day of remembering and celebrating my daughter's life. I continued to put one foot in front of the other on this path of brokenness, finding a way to celebrate Nicole's life and New Year's Day. I founded the non-profit, *Remember Me Always* and created the podcast, *Stories of Hope*. Each goes hand in hand. Stories of Hope has been my biggest achievement of honoring Nicole's life by being the example of life after tragedy, sharing how we can still live with loss and help others share their stories to either help, heal, inspire, educate or give hope.

Although my life has been permanently altered and I live a different "norm", I have no regrets. Because of my journey I am able to be a positive example. I am passionate about inspiring others. Everyone has a story that can help, heal, inspire and give hope. Through my podcast, Stories of Hope, I have met some amazing individuals who share their stories of strength, courage and hope.

W.O.W. - Words of Wisdom

Just because something different has happened to you, doesn't mean you have to be treated differently, act differently or live differently.

-    **Christine Hotchkiss**

I am not sure what hardships, devastations or losses you have had to endure, but let me encourage you: regardless of what has been lost, there can still be hope and purpose in the life that is left to live. Find a community of support that can strengthen, encourage and inspire you to live one day at a time.

Christine Hotchkiss believes we all have a walk of life that is different from one another. Some have experienced tragedy, illness, loss and life-changing situations that either help them discover their purpose, or help someone else in need.

Christine's life stories from an early age through New Year's Day 2007, when the life she once knew was changed forever. Her new "norm" has allowed her to connect with many others when it comes to sharing their journeys and enjoying the entity we call life. Christine's journey had her searching for answers and gaining certifications in Grief Recovery and Life Coaching.

She can be contacted at:
Christine@RememberMeAlways.org.
Website: www.RememberMeAlways.org

DEPRESSION MASKED AS HAPPINESS

By: Sofia L. Gonzalez

* * *

This chapter is dedicated to all the Passionistas who are striving to elevate their passion and profit by defining their identity and being who God created them to be.

Identity. As I reflect on the past, that word brings to mind many defining moments in life, where knowing who you are is essential to the evolution of who you are becoming. If we do not define ourselves, someone else—or our circumstances—will. We are living in a world where we are labeled and generalized into boxes that we have checked off at doctor's appointments or voter registration events. Our society creates stories that are not valid for everyone, speaking volumes about our outcomes. Growing up while not truly knowing your identity lays a foundation of confusion, causing people to label themselves as "not good enough" early on. Our inner dialogue questions: *Why can't I be like that person?* or *Why can't I fit in?*

I was born in Miami, and of Puerto Rican descent. However, the tanned hue of my skin led others to assume that I was African American. Moving to Ohio as a child and attending a primarily Caucasian school brought quite the contrast of labels. I was labeled as "black," then labeled as a "minority"; I was labeled "rich" while having to sign up for 20 cent meal programs, then labeled "poor" while actually doing financially well. So not being black, but Latina—yet being considered too dark to be one, I ended up in a community where I "stood out" for various reasons; one can only imagine the confidence I developed as a child. Being a pastor's daughter at the same time brought its own set of community expectations. The community cast projections that led to backlash if I fell short, because after all, for some reason … I had to be "perfect."

This undue pressure forced me to try to fit in; I tried to change myself in order to feel loved and accepted. This eventually manifested itself into a battle of low self-esteem. All the while, as I excelled in my God-given gifts and talents, I often found myself shrinking my wins so as to not outshine my peers. I won singing competitions, awards in journalism and consistently pursued the big dreams and vision God placed in my heart…secretly. I hid achievements to avoid further rejection, ostracization, insult and bullying.

It takes courage to face and truly be transparent about the most painful parts of our past—in my case, the traumatic experiences. Trauma, laced with sexual abuse and a few rapes. I hid the shame, guilt and the nightmares in masks called "joy," "happiness," "extroversion," "being happy-go-lucky" and "being light." I was a chameleon by day and haunted by my bad dreams by night. Singing praises during worship service, attending personal development courses, one after another, falling into non-Christian practices, anything… ANYTHING to numb the drowning sense that

I was of no value. Because…how could someone like me have any value with all the things I had been through? There's been countless situations where men looked at me and treated me like a commodity.

I felt like I was never good enough, but I certainly gave some of the best advice. I myself couldn't follow it at the time. The silent burden I carried of my trauma weighed heavier on my soul with each passing day. One can only continue such an existence until the dam bursts, and burst it did. I decided to tell the truth of what happened to me. But instead of being met with compassion, I was berated with judgment. Rather than understanding me, others found blame. Looking back, I now see that I was looking for acceptance from others instead of realizing one of the most powerful truths: acceptance and healing had to start with me. It was the hardest, most gruesome internal journey I'd ever have to take, but it was the best thing that's ever happened to me.

My greatest breakdown became the start of a breakthrough… I met my Maker, or should I say, GOD met me at a place where I could no longer carry myself. Where the words of gurus and personal development had failed to reach the crevices that hurt, GOD's Word started addressing the pain. I found myself divulged in a life of prayer—communicating, crying, screaming, repenting and the scariest part of all...SURRENDERING. It was the only thing left for me to do. I had no other choice, because prior choices only led to more suffering. I realized that surrendering doesn't just happen once. Surrendering comes in layers, just like an onion. When you get to the core of where the traumas lie, you are able to allow the Holy Spirit to heal the inner child wounds that only He can heal. I'd like to say this part of the journey was easy, but it was not. It was filled with the temptation to go back to who I was, and that is why it's called a spiritual battleground.

To whoever is reading this, I want you to know that prayer does work! I am not talking about affirmations to the universe or doing specific rituals and practices. I am talking about conversations with GOD, pouring your heart out and really learning about HIM in this beautiful book of His Living Word called the Bible. On the other hand, almost every personal development book has borrowed truths and regurgitated their version of it. When you read His word, you get the chance to know who He is and who YOU are in Him. You get to read stories that help you embrace all that you have been through, because nothing is new under the sun (Ecclesiastes 1:9); you get to read scriptures to help you endure where you are now, and get the guidance you need to move towards your purpose.

In order for me to really embrace my differences and accept who I was, I had to *change* my beliefs about my identity, the labels society tried to place on me and the old limiting stories that kept playing in my head. They no longer served me. I had to ask myself the hard question: *Who am I?* The first thought that came to mind was that I am a child of God. I had to claim my identity in Christ as the Daughter of the Most High King. I had to realize that I was born for a purpose. *Do not be conformed to this world, but be transformed by the renewal of your mind, that by testing you may discern what is the will of God, what is good and acceptable and perfect.* Romans 12:2, ESV

I also had to define who I am and who I am **NOT.** Say this with me: *I am not the negative things that a coach, boss, parent, sibling or teacher told me at a young age. I am not what happened to me, the rejection I faced, the past mistakes I made, the limiting beliefs I've held on to or the failures that play like a movie on repeat. I am not what I do, and my work does not define me. That is what I do, but that is not who I am.*

Passionista, I want to make this clear. Your identity is not what you do for a living. Remind yourself it is not in the success you have had, in the failures you have experienced, the mistakes you have made, your past or what someone told or said about you. Once you have reclaimed your identity and declared what you are *not*, God can begin to heal the orphan spirit within to help you claim who you really are.

Read this out loud and say it with me...

I am a daughter of the King. ----------- 1 Peter 2:9

I am God's Masterpiece. ----------------- Ephesians 2:10

I am remarkably made. ------------------ Psalm 139:14

I am worth more than rubies. ---------- Proverbs 31:10

I am always on God's mind. ----------- Psalms 139:13

I am more than a conqueror. ----------- Romans 8:31

I am strong and courageous. ----------- Deuteronomy 31:6

See, I realized that I needed to stop trying to fit in, and embrace my differences. This journey led me on the path to defining who I am, uncovering why I am here and discovering my purpose and passion. As I grew in my entrepreneurial purpose, I was able to turn my passion into profit through personal branding.

> *You have been set apart as holy to the LORD your God, and he has chosen you from all the nations of the earth to be his own special treasure.*
>
> Deuteronomy 14:2, NLT

When you think about building a legacy, your personal brand is an asset that brings back dividends and lives on even after you die. Once you declare who you are in the world, you attract a tribe that resonates with your unique story, personality and gift. That's why I am so passionate about helping other women identify who they are, why they are here and develop how they want to show up in the world. I do this through *Passionista*, a women empowerment coaching brand through my company, Affluence Media Agency. It is so easy to try to be like someone else, but it takes courage to unmask yourself and stand firm in who you are in Him.

There are 3 Keys I want you to remember in your journey of unmasking yourself:

1: It's okay to admit you are not okay. In the world of social media that perfects the imperfect conditions with filters, lighting and poses.... Go RAW! Raw enough to admit you need help and you are not perfect.

2:   GOD-fidence trumps every single, temporary, chemically-induced temporary state of escape, trend, hype or craze. There is one absolute truth to your existence and that is YOU ARE NOT A MISTAKE.

3:   The natural gifts and talents with which you have been born, the trauma you have survived and the healing of GOD weaponizes your experiences into a powerful testimony of purpose. I have built a business that helps clients identify their brand and truth. In between pain and redemption, I found out who I was—and what I saw is how HE sees me and you, as someone called worthy, forgiven, beloved and chosen.

Self-love goes beyond spa retreats, massages, make-up and materialism. It, however, is accepting your flaws and forgiving yourself and others who have wronged you, while being loving enough to impact others' lives positively. HIS word says to love others as you love yourself, not as a selfish focus, nor as a quest for perfectionism that inevitably leads to failure but as a commitment to honor. Honor the temple that is your body, your values, your life, HIM and build relationships that truly matter.

<u>W.O.W. - Words of Wisdom</u>

Ask yourself this question: "How would I like to be remembered?"
The answer lies in your true identity, your legacy.

Show up as the true Passionista within. Stand BOLDLY in who you are in Him. You get to define your story from this point on. You get the opportunity to use your story and impact others who need to hear your testimony. You in turn, build Kingdom Legacy that impacts the next generation.

You did not choose me, but I chose you and appointed you that you should go and bear fruit and that your fruit should abide, so that whatever you ask the Father in my name, he may give it to you.

– John 15:16, NKJV

Sofia Gonzalez is a Host, Speaker, Podcast Host, Brand Personality and Brand & Business Strategist. She is founder of Passionista LLC and the Purpose | Passion | Profit Summit. She has been in business since 2012 with her first company called I Am Creates You!, a Branding Agency that was rebranded into Affluence Media Agency. Sofia helps established coaches, consultants, thought leaders, and entrepreneurs elevate their passion and create a profitable brand that people know, love, and trust. Sofia has helped companies like Universal Studios, Disney, D'latinos Magazine, Univision, Florida Gulf Coast University, The Cardones, and Industry Fashion Show. Sofia has also worked with medical practices, speakers, and consultants to help them get the advantages of branding in their marketing strategy.

Instagram: @ElevateYourPassion @AffluenceMedia
www.affluencemediaagency.comwww.sofialgonzalez.comwww.purposepassionprofitsummit.com
Sofia@sofialgonzalez.com

There is Another In the Fire

By: Nephetina Serrano

Getting married young is never easy, but my husband Richard and I were in love and thriving. Yes, we had been through our share of ups and downs while building our spiritual, relational and financial foundation. We both were working at jobs that had growth potential, building our American dream. Most of all, we did our best to honor God in all things. So when the Lord opened doors for promotion at our jobs and then later provided us a once in a lifetime opportunity to move from an inner-city apartment complex to build a custom-made dream home in a surrounding state, we were elated. All of our hard work and believing in God had paid off and He was rewarding our faith. Little did we know that while embarking on the vision of our dream house, we would be at the precipice of one of the hardest seasons of trial in our life to date. Let me go back to where it all began.

I had been working a stable job with the government for six years, when I got the opportunity to become an Executive Administrative Support to one of the Senior VPs of a prominent firm. I was ambitious, hardworking and optimistic, and I applied that winning attitude to every work environment in which I had the opportunity to prove myself. I saw the position as one of significance and prestige; I considered myself as someone that always kept my eyes peeled for opportunities for advancement. So,

I was actually surprised when my boss of two and a half years recommended that I apply for a leadership position within a pilot program that the company was initiating. Honored by his high regard for me and my potential for leadership, I applied and got the position! With a pay raise, an exciting new department and a heart elated with optimism, I was beyond grateful to God. Richard and I both were making good money coupled with healthy 401ks and credit scores that were progressively repaired from the 400s to the 800s. After searching for a new home, we were finally in a position to build our own, custom-made dream home in an up-and-coming development in Delaware.

I could hardly contain my excitement. To top it off, me and Richard were renewing our vows celebrating our 15th wedding anniversary with a dream wedding vow renewal. With an elaborate ceremony, we invested $20,000 into this sacred milestone of our lives. All the while, we were able to pick and plan everything within an inch for the construction of our home. From choosing the appliances and the color of the interior and exterior of the home, to the custom molding on the walls and ceilings, we meticulously selected every detail of the home to reflect our liking. What an amazing experience that I will never forget! It was a dream come true, a fairy tale couldn't do it justice because our story reflected the hard work, blood, sweat and tears of our journey. I was as awestruck as the Israelites must have been when God delivered them from the slave huts of Egypt to the exodus journey of The Promised Land. I was sure we were entering our milk and honey season. But like the

Israelites, we had no idea of the wilderness experience that preceded the promise. If we had to admit, we did see small signs of the firestorms that were approaching. But honestly we chose to ignore them; they were minor and inconsequential to the big picture, or so we thought.

It started with the passing of my grandfather. I was very fond of him, but in his last years I did not know that he required home care in his final days. After he had passed, I learned that he had left an inheritance to me in the form of an annuity that he did not tend to regularly in the years before his death. In a manner of months before receiving my impending inheritance, a family member received the inheritance in its entirety predicated on the stipulation that once received, the money would be redistributed based on my grandfather's wishes. To my dismay, that family member reduced my predisposed inheritance to almost nothing, without as much as an apology. I was hurt more than anything, but that money would have at least been a nest egg for savings or a down payment for our home.

When it rained, it poured and the firestorm ensued. Things were going great at my job, and suddenly our department was notified that changes were being made within the company; the pilot program would subsequently end immediately. I figured that I would be able to assume my previous role supporting the Senior Vice President. However, that role had been filled in my absence, and no other eligible roles were available to me. Within a week of receiving the keys to our brand-new, custom-made dream home, I was laid off from my job.

I would receive a hefty severance package. This caused me not to go into full alarm mode in the situation. After all, I had time on my side, great references, and excellent work history, was a hard worker and was degreed. However, the job market in Delaware where we lived was not favorable, and I found myself unable to find viable employment opportunities.

This was also within weeks of our wedding extravaganza. The celebration was beautiful and exquisite, and although it was costly, Richard had picked up a part time job at a local newspaper to supplement his full-time income. Our income was somewhat stretched to pay our usual bills along with the newer wedding bills we had acquired within those months, but we were making it. We also secured a storefront for a personalized trophy business venture which was growing slowly as an additional stream of income. But without me being able to secure a job to help financially, our nest egg and savings reserve were depleting slowly. And seven fateful and grueling years later, we handed the keys to our beautiful custom-made dream home back to the bank in foreclosure. To add insult to injury, even though payment plans were arranged for both of our vehicles, both were impounded by another bank in the same week, ironically on Valentine's Day.

We were devastated. Heart-broken. Humiliated even though only those close to us knew that we were struggling financially. We still served in ministry at our church in Delaware. We still sowed and gave to others in their time of need. We painted every wall of that home, fed the neighbors and I held sleepovers for the young ladies in my area. We were the well-respected, go-to couple. We still encouraged our church family and friends. No one could tell by the smiles we offered and the suits we wore, that we were broken and beyond discouraged. Everything we had worked so hard for, had seemingly slipped through our hands, one after another. And if we hadn't lost enough, we lost our storefront because the owner of the property decided to repurpose the office space, forcing us to convert to a home-based business.

God was still with us and did not let us fall. By His grace, we were able to rent a three-bedroom townhouse in a rural area, owned by a Christian who owned various investment properties. The owner loved us and allowed us to move in immediately. Was the house beautiful? Yes. But was it our custom-made home? no. Were we still struggling workwise? Yes, Richard was still working two jobs and I was still fighting hard to secure a job as well. We started to feel the toll of this uphill battle and the rug of life was pulled from under us. It was too much to keep fighting all of it at the same time, every day. We could stomach losing our home. Our cars. Our business. But the last thing we lost was our strength. This was more than a case of embarrassment. Everything that we had worked hard for, prayed for, saved for. GONE. Just years ago, we had the American dream: to be entrepreneurs and have good jobs, and it was all gone within two years.

The stock market crashed, and the housing market was in total disarray. All of our bank account savings were depleted, our credit score had plummeted back to the 400s, and the crazy thing was half of the people that we knew and saw on a daily or weekly basis, had no idea what was going on.

It was in this devastation that my husband and I found ourselves sitting in a parking lot, ready to take our own lives. We no longer wanted to live. We had lost all hope. To make this the darkest season we had experienced to date, we no longer had the individual strength to encourage each other. Usually when one of us was down, the strong one would encourage the weaker one back to life. Like Joseph in the Bible, we had gone from the proverbial palace to the pit. But in the depths of this pit, there was no ladder in sight. No stairs winding to the entrance. There was only a little pit hole provided so we could breathe, but not enough to provide light. We simply found it hard to breathe and we didn't want to do life anymore. In that parking lot, my husband looked at me with tears rolling down his eyes. Our hearts had been ripped out of our bodies. He asked me if I was ready. I nodded. We were both ready to die.

I wish I could say it got better that day. That at that moment where we no longer wanted to live, there was a miraculous course of events that propelled us from our pit to our promise. But there were many hard days after that one. And the change was not immediate. But it did happen.

I eventually got a new job. We eventually would build again. An uphill climb, one foothold above the other. We used our resources to climb out of that storm of fire and received the help that came. There were key steps that helped us climb out of that dark place. Whatever *your* dark place, because they will eventually come, tuck these steps away in your heart so that you can use them to get through the firestorms of life.

1. **Listen to God and wait for Him to speak back to You.**

   Many times we tell God the things we want, without waiting for His response on how to move forward. In those times, our desires may line up with His, however, everything must be done in season and order. Without those key components, the "right things" may turn into stumbling blocks.

2. **Acknowledge your mistakes.**

   I can't say that I didn't recognize some of the signs to move differently, but honestly, I ignored them and hoped for the best. Could we have spaced those major events and purchases in our life differently, allowing proper time to save and build savings in between? Yes. Could we have sought help for saving our home before the foreclosure was unavoidable? Yes. Hindsight is 20/20, but moving in step with God is true wisdom.

3. **Repent.**

   Once you realize that you could have moved differently, repent. Repenting is acknowledging your wrong and turning from it, asking the Holy Spirit for wisdom in how to move forward HIS way.

4. **Forgive yourself.**

Don't beat yourself up in guilt and shame, that's a trick of the enemy. Don't allow a season of failure to define the totality of your life. Love yourself as God does and move forward in grace and wisdom.

5. **Accept help.**

If someone throws you a rope to lift you out of your pit, take it. Don't stay in the place of embarrassment and pity; move forward.

6. **Whatever you do, don't turn around.**

Refuse to look back. Praise God for every little victory, keeping your spirits up and eyes to the hills from which comes your help.

As my husband and I embarked on our 30th anniversary several years ago, I had to sit back and marvel at God's faithfulness in all circumstances. Although we are not exempt from life's ups and downs, we have overcome the pain of many pits and have gone on to experience the pleasure of our promises throughout our lifetime. With careful planning and maintenance, we garnished the wisdom to safeguard ourselves from many of the financial hardships we experienced back then. No matter the pit, palace, promise or the fires in between, God has never failed us, not one day. At times, we must go through the fires of life, but He promises that He will never leave nor forsake us. The scripture says that no weapon formed against us shall prosper, but it never said that the weapon would not form. That scripture means through it all, God will never abandon us. Regardless of the gain or loss, we have Him. And when we have Him, we have everything we need to move forward in spite of the fire.

'Look!' he answered, 'I see four men loose, walking in the midst of the fire; and they are not hurt, and the form of the fourth is like the Son of God.'

— **Daniel 3:25, NKJV**

When the three Hebrew boys decided not to bow to the king as if he was God, an infuriated King Nebuchadnezzar threw them into a fiery furnace. This fire should have killed them within seconds, but they were unharmed. Seeing this result as some type of anomaly, the king commanded that the heat of the fire be increased, to the point where it accidentally burned those responsible for throwing the three in the fire. Still, the Hebrew boys remained unscathed. Nevertheless, the heat of the fire brought them to their knees. Finally, one of King Nebuchadnezzar's minions commented that not only were the three still visibly alive in the fire, but there seemed to be a fourth in the fire with them: the Son of God.

Be encouraged! Regardless of the fire you have gone through, are in or have emerged from, Jesus is faithful to walk with you through it all. He will never leave or forsake you, and nothing shall separate you from His love. You can make it! And after the fire, there is promotion! My husband and I are living witnesses. You shall survive and live to see the goodness of the Lord. Move forward in faith and don't look back.

Dr. Nephetina L. Serrano is an Evangelist, International Empowerment Speaker, Marriage Counselor, Certified Life-Coach, #1 International Best Selling Author, 4xs Amazon Best Seller, Publisher and Mentor.

She is Co-founder of Covenant Marriages, Covenant Rescue 911, and Covenant Marriages Institute. She supports couples in crisis. Dr. Nephetina and husband Dr. Richard Serrano Co-host their show "Your Marriage Matters" She co-authored the book, THE MARRIAGE CORPORATION which highlights the organizational needs of a covenant marriage. She is the Publisher of Marriage CEO Magazine, "For the Entrepreneur Who Leads, Building Legacy."

Dr. Serrano has received many awards and certificates including; City of Philadelphia CITATION Women of Wealth, "Publishers Golden Eagle Award" Success Magazine named her as one of the 100 Best Life Coaches 2021, State of California SENATE Recognition in honor of GSFE County of Riverside Influencer Award and more.

www.marriageCEOs360.com / DrSerranoministries@gmail.com

116 BALA AVE, SUITE 1B, BALA CYNWYD, PA 19004